Red Children in White America

Red Children
in
White America

Ann H. Beuf

University of Pennsylvania Press/1977

Library of Congress Cataloging in Publication Data

Beuf, Ann H   1938-
    Red children in white America.

    Bibliography: p.
    Includes index.
    1. Indians of North America--Ethnic identity.
2. Race awareness. 3. Indians of North America--
Children. I. Title.
E98.E85B48   301.45'19'7073   76-49737
ISBN 0-8122-7719-8

Printed in the United States of America

———◆◆———

To Native American children—
the Red Power of tomorrow.

———◆◆———

Contents

List of Tables

Acknowledgments

While it is impossible to list all of the people who have made valuable contributions to this book, I would like to express my gratitude to the following: to the Ford Foundation for funding the initial fieldwork; to the Guttman Foundation for making the time in which to work available; to Margaret Tashquinth, Shirley Cayou, Oliver Sansoci and Vivian One Feather for their hospitality and their help with the research; to Margot Liberty who contributed a wealth of background information as well as a roof over my head in Nebraska; to Eugene V. Schneider and Renée C. Fox for their critical readings of the manuscript; to Bob Erwin of the University of Pennsylvania Press who has been constructively critical and most supportive; to Magoli S. Larson and Chek Beuf for their continual support and interest in the progress of the work; to Honey, Carlo and Peter Beuf who endured the rigors of fieldwork without complaint; to Martha Rosso for an interested typing of the manuscript; to Shelley Block for one hundred assorted tasks accomplished. I would like to acknowledge especially the contribution of Judith Porter, teacher, advisor, critic and friend, without whose instruction and encouragement this book would not have been written.

CHAPTER 1

Introduction

———◆◆◆———

This is a study of racial attitudes in Native American pre-school children and a control group of white children.[1] Although our nation has within its borders nearly one million Native Americans, until recently sociological and psychological research in the field of race relations has revolved almost exclusively around black-white relations. The past decade in particular witnessed a growth in the body of research on racial attitudes inspired by the early Civil Rights and later Black Power movements.

1. The term Native American will be used throughout the book. It is the name which many of those commonly known as American Indians prefer to apply to their own group. "Indian," after all, is a misnomer—the result of Columbus's mistaken belief that he had reached the shores of India. As such, it is a relic of European "colonial" influence.

In contrast to the black, who has been studied within the context of twentieth-century, industrial America, the Native American has been the subject of social science research from an historical perspective, as heir to a colorful past rather than in his present status as a member of an oppressed minority group. (One thinks of the way the social scientists seem to divide the labor, as if some invisible authority had given blacks to sociologists and social psychologists, while allocating Native Americans to historians and anthropologists.) Most anthropological research has attempted to reconstruct Native American customs from the accounts of tribal members, or to discuss present situations in terms of "deculturation." Margaret Mead's work on the Omaha, the studies of the Indian Education Research Project in the forties, Murray Wax's *Indian Americans*, and the contributors to Bahr, Chadwick, and Day's *Native Americans Today* are notable exceptions.[2] However, many of these studies were conducted before World War II and much has transpired since then to bring far-reaching changes to the lives of most Native Americans. The fantastic growth of industry which has characterized the postwar period, the spread of communication and transportation networks, the influence of the Civil Rights movement, and the rise of Red Power have brought enormous changes to Native American life and thus demand a body of research that treats Native Americans within the present historical context. Hopefully, this will be but one of many works which seek to broaden the field of race relations to include the Native American group.

In the past few years, as a result of national attention

2. Margaret Mead, *The Changing Culture of an Indian Tribe* (New York: Columbia University Press, 1946); Gordon Macgregor, *Warriors without Weapons* (Chicago: University of Chicago Press, 1946); Alice Joseph, Rosamund Spicer, and Jane Chesky, *The Desert People* (Chicago: University of Chicago Press, 1949); Murray Wax, *Indian Americans, Unity and Diversity* (Englewood Cliffs, N.J.: Prentice-Hall, 1971); and Howard Bahr, Bruce A. Chadwick and Robert C. Day, *Native Americans Today: Sociological Perspectives* (New York: Harper and Row, 1972).

focused on the "Indian problem," there has been a heightened awareness of the economic deprivation suffered by Native Americans and the difficulties inherent in their relationship to white society. Unfortunately, all too often when researchers have focused on the present-day Native American their interest has been in the deviant. Here the Native American is seen as "the drunk," or "the suicide." While such persons do exist in Native American societies, sometimes in alarming proportions, they are not the majority, and their story does not tell us about the thousands of Native Americans who lead day-to-day lives void of pathology. More research is needed on nondeviant Native Americans, and their relationship to the dominant white society.

Nor should such research focus exclusively on adults. By now it is well known that racial feelings are established at an early age.[3] Furthermore, psychologists who may disagree on a plethora of theoretical issues are in accord on the importance of early childhood experience. Feelings about race formed early in childhood are bound to color adult race relations. For this reason, it is important to learn what attitudes Native American children hold about their own racial group, and to investigate the contribution of cultural and social factors to these attitudes.

Our aim is to investigate whether the Native American children's attitudes are indeed different from those of a control group of white children, and, if so, what may be the social sources of such differences. How does the Native American child see his or her race? How is he or she influenced by the white concepts of "beauty" and "goodness" brought by television, pictures in magazines and books, exposure to white teachers or VISTA workers, and the conversations of those in his or her environment?

In a broader vein, the study also addresses itself to a question of concern to those interested in race-relations theory.

3. See, for example, Judith D. R. Porter, *Black Child, White Child* (Cambridge: Harvard University Press, 1971).

This is the relative importance in the formation of the minority-group child's racial concepts of the two phenomena which I shall designate (1) prejudicial discrimination and (2) institutional racism.

In a situation of prejudicial discrimination, the individual incurs psychological abuse—or hurt feelings—through some felt attitude or overt action on the part of others related to their negative feelings about the minority group. Institutional racism is more subtle, "the byproduct of certain institutional practices which operate to restrict on a racial basis the choices, rights, mobility and access of groups of individuals."[4] Cultural racism exists when racist images permeate beliefs, norms, and values, or when a group is not present at all in the culture, having been excluded.[5] Table 1 gives illustrations of these concepts.

To be affected by institutional racism, the child need be only a sensitive observer of the social situation.

Most studies of children's racial attitudes have assumed that it was prejudicial discrimination which caused whatever undesirable attitudes were found in minority-group subjects. Yet recent studies of children's ability to understand a "pecking order" and to comprehend political events[6] indicate that, at an early age, children begin to understand social arrangements and hierarchies. It may be comprehension of these social and political factors which shapes racial attitudes. The child's cognition would thus be of more importance in this process than has been realized.

It would be quite difficult to determine the relative weights of prejudicial discrimination and institutional and cultural racism on the attitudes of black children, because, to a large

4. James M. Jones, *Prejudice and Racism* (Reading, Mass.: Addison-Wesley, 1972), p. 6.

5. Ibid.

6. See, for example, Melvin De Fleur and Lois B. De Fleur, "The Relative Contribution of Television as a Learning Source for Children's Occupational Knowledge," *American Sociological Review* 32 (1967): 777-89.

Table 1

Prejudicial discrimination and institutional-cultural racism

Explanation	Example	Aspects of Minority Reality
1. Traumatic name-calling and social rejection	"nigger" "I don't want to sit beside that brown girl."	Prejudice and active discrimination, experienced by individual.
2. Observation of the society's role structure, realization that minorities fall below whites in the hierarchy	Child sees teachers are Indian, head teacher is white. The social worker is white; she can tell mother what to do. Daddy gets dirty at work. White men wear clean shirts and tell Daddy what to do.	Institutional-cultural racism.

extent, they are subject to both influences simultaneously. However, reservation Native American youngsters are relatively isolated from the prejudicial discrimination factor, having little contact with whites. This is especially true of preschool youngsters who stay close to mother or grandmother and thus avoid the one-to-one relations with whites which older children encounter on shopping or recreational expeditions.

The children who took part in this study were 229 preschoolers—117 Native Americans and 95 whites. The Native American children come from three different tribal groups whose histories and life-styles are described in depth in chapter 2. Fifty-five are from a tribe whose ancient agricultural lands lie to the south of Phoenix, Arizona. Twenty are from a Dakota plains tribe. The other group, a former hunting-gathering plains group of the upper Missouri, is divided into reservation and urban subsamples. Half of these children reside on their tribal reservation of rolling Nebraska farmland, while the others are residents of Lincoln, Nebraska.

Institutional and cultural racism permeate the lives of all Native Americans. To whatever institution one looks, the reins of power are in white hands. In politics, economics, education, and health, while there may be Native Americans involved, the final decisions are always made by whites. With the coming of radio and television to the reservation, today's children, more than any other generation of Native Americans, receive early exposure to the social system of this country. With the exception of a few token representatives of the Native Americans—most often cast in the role of "the enemy"—the people they see are white or perhaps black. The decision makers appear to be mostly white.

This situation permits us to examine the relative importance of prejudicial discrimination and institutional and cultural racism in determining children's racial feelings. Sheltered as they are from the grosser incidents of prejudicial discrimination, Native American children might be expected to evince few feelings of discomfort concerning their racial status. At least, such would be the hypothesis of those who have assumed that such feelings originate in the child's coming face to face with such incidents. However, the central hypothesis of this study is that institutional and cultural racism alone make themselves felt in the life of the isolated reservation child, imparting the awareness of white dominance to him or her at an early age. Thus there are three main tasks before us, the first of which is to establish that cultural and institutional racism do exist with regard to Native Americans, and that they have a profound influence on the lives even of rather isolated reservation children.

Our culture is riddled through with anti-Native American beliefs and values. The insensitivity with which the Native American image is treated is accentuated when we contrast the new sensitivity of the American public to the black image. Amos 'n' Andy are gone but Tonto continues to "ugh" and "how" his way into the lives of millions of children.

Halloween provides another example. No parent who considers himself a right-minded American would blacken his child's face, and give him an Afro wig and calico shirt for trick-or-treating, yet every October 31 the streets fill with children in moccasins, breech-cloths, feathers, and war paint. In short, the culture conspires to make a joke or a threat of Native Americans.

As Gordon Allport noted, language itself can help form prejudicial images simply by imbuing words with symbolic meaning which becomes associated both with an unpleasant idea and a minority group of people.[7] Thus black is associated with sin, the terrors of night and death, as well as with Negroes. Red, too, is associated with unpleasant notions: with blood, a fearful concept in childhood when it is seen in times of pain, with anger ("seeing red"), and recently with a new "enemy," Communism.

An Indian-giver is one who takes back what he has given (although Indian generosity is legendary). People speak of "going on the warpath" with regard to pursuing an angry course, and the preparations a woman makes for sexual conquest may be called "putting on her war paint." As for the phrase "give it back to the Indians," Vine Deloria comments: "It's a terrible thing for a people to realize that society has set aside all non-working gadgets for their exclusive use."[8] And we are all familiar with "the only good Indian is a dead Indian."

A survey by Kathleen Houts and Rosemary Bahr of stereotyping cartoons revealed that Native Americans, when portrayed, were shown in most cases wearing feathers and war paint, and engaged in shooting arrows or other warlike activity. The authors state, "The message they [magazine cartoons] convey is that the Indian in American life is important only as a

7. Gordon Allport, *The Nature of Prejudice* (Garden City, N.Y.: Doubleday Anchor Books, 1958).

8. Vine Deloria, Jr., *Custer Died for Your Sins: An Indian Manifesto* (New York: Avon Books, 1969), p. 10.

primitive, historical, bow-and-arrow type who has no place in the modern society."[9]

My own work on the image that television projects of the Native American shows that here, too, the image is one of a warring primitive, with an occasional basket weaver thrown in for "educational" value. In 1972–73, we saw only two programs which dealt with a twentieth-century Native American and the problems he faced in white society. Usually the Native American is presented, not only historically, but as "the enemy," and in television cartoons he is treated with callous humor, in the poorest taste.

Textbooks have long been a prime source of the Native American image. Lee Bowker, in a content analysis of texts, found that Native Americans, as well as blacks, are underrepresented in texts on American history, especially considering the role they have played in American life. In addition, many of the references were unfavorable and degrading.[10]

Deloria also deals with texts and points out that the few positive characters who appear, such as Squanto and some of the scouts during the Indian Wars, were traitors to their own people who facilitated white encroachment on Native American lands. Such Native Americans, Deloria says, were not really "good Indians," as the texts would have it, but simply Native Americans as the white man wants them to be—strong, friendly, and subservient. In this context, he cites the fictional Tonto, companion to the Lone Ranger, dumb, monosyllabic, and always *there*, placing him in the same category as the devoted Negro butler and the Japanese gardener—also white creations.[11] The same could be said of the Native American

9. Kathleen Houts and Rosemary Bahr, "Stereotyping of Indians and Blacks in Magazine Cartoons," in Bahr, Chadwick, and Day, *Native Americans Today*, pp. 110-14.

10. Lee H. Bowker, "Red and Black in Contemporary American History Texts: A Content Analysis," in Bahr, Chadwick, and Day, *Native Americans Today*, pp. 101-09.

11. Deloria, *Custer Died for Your Sins*, pp. 9-34.

friend of the protagonist of James Fenimore Cooper's *Leather-stocking Tales.*

All of these factors promote a consistent and rarely chal-lenged image of the Native American as an untamed child of nature, as in one movie which I analyzed, in which the whites' accomplishments were attributed to intelligence, and those of Native Americans to "intuition." Sometimes friendly in an amusing or fawning manner, the Native American is more often depicted as an enemy, frightening as well as inspiring feelings of white superiority.

It seems unnecessary for the purposes of this study to ex-plore the existence of cultural racism in greater depth. It is so apparent and so widespread that we must accept the fact that many Native American children as well as whites are exposed to negative, racist images through texts, storybooks, movies, television, figures of speech, and advertising campaigns which invoke Native Americans as mascots or trademarks.

Institutional racism and its impact on the lives of Native American children are more complex and demand thorough treatment. The history of institutional racism in Native Ameri-can life, the institutional arrangements which now shape and limit the life experiences of Native Americans, and the man-ner in which these forces act on the three groups studied during the research are discussed in chapter 2, "The World of the Native American Child." I would like to emphasize that this chapter seeks to present, in rather bold strokes, an *over-view* of the history of Native American-white relations. It does not represent an attempt to give a comprehensive his-torical account of the relations between the two groups. Anthropologists will probably find little with which they are not already familiar. However, as I have been intentionally interdisciplinary in my approach, it is necessary to supply some basic historical background for the sociologists, psy-chologists, and educators who may have great interest in the minority-group child but lack exposure to Native American history.

Our second task is to investigate and set forth the attitudes which preschool Native American children hold about racial matters and to consider how such attitudes articulate with their perception of the social order. The results of this research will be presented in chapter 3, "Racial Attitudes of Native American Children." The third and most difficult task is to suggest a theory which can incorporate empirical findings with theoretical material in such a way as to explain the observations made in this study and findings from the field of the development of children's attitudes in general. An appraisal of my own data, combined with consistent findings in other studies of children's racial attitudes, suggests the necessity for incorporating several sociological and psychological principles into a new theory of the development of racial attitudes. This effort will concern us in chapter 4, "Towards a Theory of the Development of Racial Attitudes."

The data presented in this book have been gathered from numerous sources, employing a variety of methodologies. The core of the study is the projective storytelling test and the responses of the preschool children to the test questions. However, spontaneous remarks made by the children were noted, as were the plots of the stories they made up themselves and their behavior with the test equipment. Field notes were kept on classroom behavior and special notes made of any conversation that related to race.

Informal and unstructured interviews were also carried out with parents of some of the children. Many mothers expressed interest in the project, and the conversations we had helped to give me background data on some of the children. These women conveyed to me some anecdotal material regarding the children's racial experiences, which was of immense help in developing and illustrating a theory of the development of racial attitudes.

Teachers and members of the community were also interviewed informally. These informants provided the vital sociological information needed on the community as a whole and on the individual children in particular. For instance, one of the variables which was of interest to me was parental activism. Questioning the informants about the children's parents and their roles in the community allowed me to classify children as coming from either a nonactivist home, a home in which one parent was an activist, or a home in which two parents were activists.

Participant observation also played a role in the accumulation of data. Field notes were taken on all of the communities involved in the study and every potential source of information was investigated. This involved interviews with Model Cities workers, eighty-year-old women, and those involved in the American Indian Movement. Conversations with children outside the sample also are utilized in our consideration of the material, as well as a few "serendipitous experiments" described in chapter 3.

I spent as much of my leisure time as possible with Native American people, going to supermarkets, drinking coffee, attending powwows, helping prepare for a funeral, and generally socializing. Through these activities I gained a sense of the social world in which many of the first Americans presently live. I also made some good friends with whom I have remained in contact and whom I have visited in the summers since the year in which the bulk of the research was carried out. These repeated visits have crystallized many of the impressions which appear in the section on the world of the Native American child. Sometimes things have changed, as in the dramatic acceleration of social protest on one of the reservations. I have attempted to keep up to date and to present the reader with as contemporary a portrait of Native American life-conditions as possible. In addition, I carried out a content analysis of fifty television programs to expose the media's image of Native Americans.

The library, as well as the field, has played a vital role in gathering the empirical and theoretical material essential if the book is to convey all that I hope it will. The Native American publications—in particular, *Akwesasne Notes* and *Wassaja*—have kept me constantly informed on Native American affairs in general, and on the three groups represented here in particular. Histories, ethnographies, and agents' letters all aided in the preparation of the historical and demographic sections.

Finally, through a continued involvement in Native American affairs, I have had access to that most subtle source of information—communication with peers. By moving back and forth between these informal, word-of-mouth sources and reliably documented confirmation or refutation of such messages, I have kept in close touch with events that will have an impact on the lives of my subjects.

Thus, it would be misleading to describe this study solely as a social-psychological testing of preschool children. Such a description conjures up images of an efficient "tester" who appears in the school, tests all the children, and disappears into the computer room for two weeks to emerge with a pat study ready for publication. My involvement with my subjects has been more intense than that of a tester. I have lived on their lands, read their papers, attended their conferences, attempted to tell their story to white students and the white press, rejoiced with them on victories won, trembled by the "all news" radio through the night when Nixon threatened to invade the occupied village of Wounded Knee, and felt the frustrations of those who rebelled only to see the old order re-established. The children in the study came to be my friends. Parting brought sadness on both sides.

The question of "value freedom" plagues all sociologists, but particularly those who seek primary data and thus interact directly with their subjects. No matter how hard I try, I cannot regard these children as only "data." But beyond this bias, there is the more persistent question of the political and social values of the researcher and the manner in which these might influence the selection of research topics and the interpretation of the data. I adhere to the position that value freedom is an impossibility for the sociologist. One's interests, guilts, and politics do indeed play vital roles in the selection of a topic. That is certainly the case with the present work. Values color our interpretation of the accumulated material. Measures can be taken to guard against this: for example, the selection of an unbiased sample and the use of statistical tests minimize the influence of the researcher's biases on the interpretation of data. However, these, too, can be influenced in subtle ways by one's own values. Thus the sociologist must face the inevitability of some intrusion of values into his or her work, and place the burden of objectivity on the reader by openly stating those values and letting the reader take them and their possible influence into account in assessing the arguments set forth. Therefore, I should like to present to the reader the intellectual and ideological underpinnings of this book.

The question of values is closely related to another concern, the neglect sociology has exhibited toward cognitive factors and their role in social interaction. Such neglect prevents the acquisition of a total picture of attitude formation, which thus is viewed as the product of child-rearing and traumatic childhood experiences. The child is an actor in the process of developing attitudes, not simply a receptacle into which knowledge is poured. Thus I confess to a cognitive bias in considering the children's responses to my questions. It is my belief that actual material situations which exist in the social system have as great an influence on children's perceptions of the world as do events of their inner psychological lives. For this reason I have focused on the role of institutional arrangements in the acquisition of racial attitudes.

I must confess also to a structural bias with regard to social change. Waiting to "change the hearts and minds of men" will avail us little. This book's message, if it has a single message, is that social-structural factors play a vital role in establishing negative images about one's own group, and social-structural changes must occur to change them. This book is for those who have an interest in the Native American situation in 1977, for students of race-relations theory, and for educators who are concerned with the development of children's racial attitudes. It is also a statement of my own orientation to sociology. In recent years, with an increased interest in wide-sweeping social change and macrosociology, there has been a general lack of interest in socialization and in the relationship between personality and social systems. To describe this as a lack of interest is perhaps an understatement, for there has been, in fact, a certain suspicion of, and hostility toward, those who would devote their efforts to these fields of study. It is assumed that such people are disinterested in social change, concerned with internal personality factors rather than with the institutional and other environmental factors which impinge on the consciousness of people, and, in general, lacking in humanistic and perhaps professional values. Such is not necessarily the case. To discover the effects of oppression on personality is not to place its source within the individual or to deny the absolute necessity for changing social conditions. At the level of personality we come face to face with the impact of unjust societal arrangements in an unavoidable manner. It is my belief that the study of personality has far-reaching implications for understanding the mechanisms and effects of injustice.

CHAPTER 2

The World of the
Native American Child

———◆◆———

In considering how children view their own race and the other races who make up the society in which they live, it is necessary to set forth the context in which their attitudes are being formed. Kurt Lewin's concept of "the field" has taught social scientists that most perceptions take place within a given set of circumstances and that an individual's concept of himself and others is colored by the spatial and temporal contexts in which that perception occurs.[1] To do justice to a consideration of attitudes, then, we must take seriously C. Wright Mills's mandate to regard as our subject the intersection of biography and history.

1. Kurt Lewin, *Field Theory in Social Science: Selected Theoretical Papers* (New York: Harper and Brothers, 1951).

Because so much is known about the social milieu of white children, especially by those in the fields that comprise the social and behavioral sciences, we shall concentrate on the Native American child in this chapter. What are the economic, physical, and educational characteristics of the world in which this child lives?

Generalizations about "Indians" necessarily distort the truth. Those Native Americans who deviate from the typical situation, for better or worse, do not emerge in bold relief from such an approach. I realize this and apologize to those whose life circumstances differ from the picture I will be setting forth in this chapter. I would also caution the reader to keep this in mind. The overview of Native American life presented here is based on the typical reservation situation. It does not treat the urban Native American thoroughly, nor does it deal with the nascent middle-class and professional groups. It is an "ideal type" in the Weberian sense and should be considered only as such. For example, the reader should remember that when we cite a per capita income for the Native American group, we are citing the *mean*. There are millionaire Native Americans (precious few) whose situation is obscured by such a treatment, and there are those whose poverty is such that it falls well below the mean and, indeed, is of such depth as to defy statistical description. Nonetheless, given the general lack of awareness on the part of most whites (particularly in the eastern United States) concerning Native Americans and the lives they lead, and with this caution in mind, it would still seem of benefit to describe the typical reservation situation, that the reader might better understand the responses of Native American children that will appear in the data presentation and gain some "feel" for the world as it appears to these children.

First I will briefly examine the history of Native American–white relations. Then I will present an overview of the life conditions which confront most Native Americans today. Finally, an ethnographical approach to the three groups of Native Americans who took part in this particular study will indicate how their lives fit into this general picture and are, indeed, representative of it.

An overview of the Native American experience

Bitter roots in the past

From the outset, exploitation and cultural supremacy were the hallmarks of white attitudes toward Native Americans. Greeted with friendliness, the invaders, with their growing population, soon felt the need to expand westward and proceeded to do so, removing more and more land from the inhabitants. What Native Americans regarded as the wisdom of conservation and the co-existence of man and nature was regarded as ignorance and wastefulness by the white settlers. With psyches dominated by the Protestant ethic, they rationalized and justified atrocities against Native Americans in terms of their belief that land and resources that were not being turned into something else were being improperly utilized. Thus they were not above rejoicing when disaster and plague struck the indigenous peoples, going so far as to thank God for sending smallpox to the Native Americans. These people considered the original inhabitants of the continent as somewhat lower than human beings, a species of animal. Had they known of evolution, they would doubtless have placed the Native American somewhere beneath *homo sapiens* on the evolutionary scale.[2]

Of course, white ethnocentrism is most evident in the concept of discovery itself. It is difficult to perceive how one can "discover" and lay claim to territory which is already inhabited. It is only if one considers one's own ethnic group to be

2. This tendency was evident in a display I saw in 1972 in a prominent museum in the Southwest. On one wall, the evolution of man was displayed. The progression was monkey, higher primate, Neanderthal, "Indian," and *homo sapiens,* white!

the *only* human group that one can ignore over a million people and claim such territory. Yet, to this day, white and Native American children are taught in their schools that Columbus discovered America. Such teaching is understandably confusing for Native American youngsters. This ethnocentric concept—discovery—has been the subject of a good deal of Native American humor. Perhaps an example of this humor will help white readers to understand how insulting and demeaning it is to have an entire population imagined out of existence—especially if you happen to be part of that population.

> I would say that we discovered the white man, too. At that time we hadn't known that there was land across the sea, so I think by the same token that the next time I go to England or Italy, I intend to take a flag and plant it and claim it for my Indian people, because, after all, *it would be the first time that I had ever seen it, so therefore I would be discovering it.*[3]

The accumulation of Native American land almost always took place under the guise of friendship, with treaties and the exchange of gifts. Those tribal leaders who caught on and refused to go along with the charade are those we are taught in school to regard as "bad Indians." "Good Indians," on the other hand, are those who not only befriended the whites but were traitors to their own people.

The expedient nature of white policy towards Native Americans is apparent in the history of the colonial period and the time following independence. So long as other Europeans posed a threat to the settlers, care was taken to insure alliance with Native Americans. Promises were frequently made to tribes in exchange for their assistance in warfare. These promises were just as frequently left unfulfilled once hostilities ceased. After the colonies had gained independence, and prior to the Louisiana Purchase, fear of the French kept the colonists honest. To insure the borders, friendships with

3. Anonymous, quoted in *I Have Spoken: American History through the Voices of Indians,* ed. Virginia Armstrong (New York: Pocket Books, 1972). Italics added.

strong Native American groups were formed and supported by fur-trading posts, which paid fair to very good prices. As soon as the purchase had been made and there was no external threat on the border, the posts were closed, and traders who paid unfair prices for their furs were permitted to assume the Native American trade.

The desire for land was becoming more intense, and huge profits were realized as the government bought land from the Native Americans for a pittance and resold it to whites for handsome sums. Sometimes the government realized a profit amounting to ten times what it had paid for a piece of land. This type of exploitation continued throughout the early days of the nation, as Manifest Destiny took the white man's hunger for land and sanctimonious belief in his divine right to it across the continent. Indeed, we can see signs of Manifest Destiny still: in the government's attempt to make the sacred Blue Lake of the Taos people part of a national park; in the extensive strip-mining undertaken on many reservations by large corporations; and in the state of New York's "removal" of a large portion of the Tuscarora reservation to create a reservoir.

White desire for more land for cultivation brought about the first effort at "relocating" Native Americans. Despite protest from the Supreme Court, Andrew Jackson's administration began the process of moving all the Native Americans east of the Mississippi to the western side. This was accomplished under the Indian Removal Act of 1830, with the loss of many lives on the notorious Trail of Tears. There is a particular irony involved in this event which demonstrates the extent of white racism at that time. The groups most damaged by this treaty were those known as the "civilized tribes," tribes which had gone to great lengths to accommodate the invaders. They had become first-rate farmers, spoke English as well as their own tongues, read and wrote, dressed like Europeans, and were Christianized. Yet in the final analysis this availed them little. Although white rhetoric relied on the concept of "the heathen savage" to justify the taking of lands, it mattered not at all that these people bore little resemblance to the stereotype. Their land was demanded by whites, for whites, and they were forced to move.[4]

After the Civil War, the inventions of barbed wire, the artesian well, and the repeating rifle made possible white conquest and cultivation of the Plains, which whites had not wanted before. The deliberate killing of the buffalo hastened the downfall of the powerful Plains tribes, and the bitter Indian Wars finished the process. Government policy was capricious, as alternating humane and punitive measures were proposed and initiated. The brutal treatment of early reservation Native Americans, tragically symbolized by the Wounded Knee Massacre,[5] aroused moral indignation in some quarters and genocidal determination in others. In dialectic fashion, these two responses were synthesized in the concept of assimilation. It made the moralists happy, because it was "doing good" for Native Americans to give them clothing, food, education and religion; it satisfied the genocidal faction, because the desired end-product was the disappearance of the Native American, who would be absorbed into the dominant society as his language, customs, religion, and family structure were demolished. It was a compromise policy, designed to result in the cultural, although not physical, destruction of an entire ethnic group.

The policy of assimilation was behind the boarding-school system of the day, which forbade the speaking of any lan-

4. There are still Native Americans east of the Mississippi because many had assimilated into white society and were not defined as "Indian" at the time of the act, and also because the Seminoles refused to be removed and entered into a long-enduring armed conflict with the United States government which cost the government a fortune. The Seminoles never did move west of the Mississippi.

5. A group of Sioux returning from a religious event were disarmed and shot down by government troops in 1878. Many of the victims were women and children. The bodies were left unburied and frozen on the ground for several days and then subjected to mass burial in trenches. Photographs of this event bear uncanny resemblance to those of similar events at Dachau and Auschwitz. For a complete description of the massacre, see *Bury My Heart At Wounded Knee,* by Dee Brown.

guage other than English, the outlawing of Native American religious celebrations, and the Dawes Act of 1887. This act, also known as the Allotment Act, divided Native American lands into individual parcels. The manifest reason for this was to promote assimilation and to turn the Native American into a brown replica of the white farmer. However, it is interesting to note that the act also furthered exploitation of the Native Americans' resources. First, it was found that there was a good deal of land "left over" after tribally held lands had been distributed to Native American individuals. The government opened these lands to white homesteaders instead of returning them to the tribe. In addition, the farming model, which reflected white values of individuality and the private ownership of property, was not an appealing way of life to many Native Americans.

Individual ownership in many cases brought economic disaster at the hands of the land speculators. Traditionally foreign to the concept of private property, naive and untutored in white economic dealings, possessing an ethic which valued display, sharing, and generosity over individual acquisitiveness, many Native Americans sold their allotments for what they believed to be a great deal of money. The money soon was spent, and they returned to friends and relatives penniless and without land for farming or grazing. In all, nearly one million acres were transferred from Native American to white hands as a result of the Dawes Act.

During the twenties there was a heightened realization of the poverty and poor health conditions which plagued the Native American population. Action was proposed in Congress that no land in the territory previously held by Spain would be considered legitimately held unless those upon it could produce the original land grant. Groups of white sympathizers joined with a Native American alliance to prevent the loss of land by the southwestern Native Americans, and the action was defeated.

The government commissioned Lewis Meriam to research conditions on the reservations, and the Meriam Report, com-

pleted in 1928, condemned the reservation system with a ven-
geance. It recommended the restoration of languages and reli-
gions, the cultivation of Native American leadership, and a
greater role for Native Americans in the conduct of their own
affairs.[6] The Roosevelt Administration attempted to implement the suggestions of the report, but without total success.
It fostered a return of Native American lands and halted the
further sale of such lands. It also instituted a system of loans
to tribes for the development of business enterprises and
industrial development. In addition, measures taken at this
time, to alleviate the conditions faced by the general population during the Depression also affected the Native American.
Such groups as the Papago were able to find their first employment in the Civilian Conservation Corps on or near their home
reservations.

The Eisenhower administration reversed these gains by
adopting a resolution of "termination" of the special rights and
services enjoyed by Native Americans. Some tribes were simply defined out of existence, while others, deprived of tax-
exempt status, lost all of their land.

Native Americans today

Economics

Most Native Americans are poor.[7] Per capita income ave-
rages around $1,500 a year, about one-half the national "pov-
erty level," but individual cases are often worse. On some
reservations, large families may have a total income of under
$1,000, and Native Americans tend to have large families.

6. Lewis Meriam et al., *The Problem of Indian Administration* (Baltimore: Johns Hopkins Press, 1928).
7. Most of what follows is derived from Murray Wax, *Indian Americans*; Department of Commerce, *U.S. Census of Population, 1960 (Nonwhite Population by Race)* (Washington, D.C.: Government Printing
Office, 1963); and Helen Johnson, "Rural Indian Americans in Poverty,"
in Bahr, Chadwick and Day, *Native Americans Today*, pp. 24-30.

The birth rate is considerably higher than that of the country as a whole, and the traditional extended family still prevails in many places. Therefore, when we are talking about such low incomes, we may be talking about a group of ten or twelve people who must survive on these sub-poverty level earnings.[8]

Not only is income low, but when we examine the sources of Native American income we find that a large part of it comes from government assistance, veterans' aid, land leases, and government employment. It is difficult for Native Americans to obtain ordinary nongovernment employment. This is partly because most reservations are well out of commuting range of the better employment markets. It is also due to lack of education at a time when arbitrary standards are set for hiring, such as the requirement of a high-school diploma for work on an assembly line. Lack of training in the more marketable skills in a changing economy is also a handicap as machines take over many of the tasks for which antiquated technical schools have trained Native American youth. We should also note that discrimination in hiring practices plays an important role in limiting the availability of good employment for Native Americans. There is little doubt that white prejudice exists, although few studies, since the early Bogardus studies, have systematically examined attitudes towards Native Americans. Bogardus showed that the unfavorable image of Native Americans was not changing at the same rate as prejudice towards other groups in society. In the area of social-distance prejudice, for instance, prejudice towards Native Americans increased between 1946 and 1956, while negative attitudes towards other groups showed a decrease in this respect.[9] In a study of anti-Native American prejudice in a Colorado mining town, Ralph Luebben noted that prejudice

8. Of course the extended family can be an asset, and some have argued that it is indeed the merit of combined income which has perpetuated that family structure among Native Americans.

9. Emory Bogardus, "Racial Distance," in *Sociological Analysis: An Empirical Approach through Replication,* ed. Murray A. Strauss and Joel I. Nelson (New York: Harper and Row, 1968), pp. 276-81.

was accompanied by discrimination in hiring and in admission to community organizations, such as the Boy Scouts.[10] Joseph, Spicer, and Chesky note that the general public in the area near a reservation look upon Native American people as a lower-class group with a tendency towards drunkenness, and, though they are not subjected to as marked social discrimination as Negroes, they must endure a certain amount of racial prejudice.[11]

Macgregor's analysis of white attitudes is more sophisticated because he considers the effects of social class on intergroup attitudes.

> To sum up, attitudes vary generally with the social status of the white man. The tradespeople, well-to-do farmers and government employees who form the middle class of South Dakota and Nebraska, look upon most Indians as socially and economically inferior. The Indians who are acceptable to this group are those whose education, employment and social behavior are like their own. There is, however, another group of whites in the area to whom the Indians, especially the mixed bloods, are more acceptable, and with whom there is some inter-marriage. This group is largely composed of the poorer farmers and townspeople, often those who live on "the wrong side of the tracks."[12]

Mead noted little real social contact between the "Antlers" and the whites of towns near their reservation. "The distribution of whites and Indians over the same territory does not make for much contact between races. The two groups live separate lives, often curiously centered about the same event."[13] Thus, even a well-trained and educated Native American has problems gaining employment close to home. The result is an unemployment rate which is nearly twice the

10. Ralph A. Luebben, "Prejudice and Discrimination against Navajos in a Mining Community," in Bahr, Chadwick and Day, *Native Americans Today*, pp. 89-101.

11. Joseph, Spicer, and Chesky, *The Desert People*, pp. 191-221.

12. Macgregor, *Warriors without Weapons*, pp. 205-09.

13. Mead, *Changing Culture*, p. 36.

white average, and which on individual reservations has been known to run as high as 70 percent. In the city, Native Americans, like blacks, tend to be "last hired, first fired."

Making a living on the reservation, without working for the government or the Bureau of Indian Affairs (BIA), is also difficult. The land given Native Americans at the time the reservations were set out was land whites believed to be useless.[14] Therefore Native Americans live on some of the most nonarable, nongrazable land in the country. Water may be hard to come by, as white farmers and ranchers divert it for their own purposes. This makes irrigation virtually impossible. In addition, the Native American farmer faces all the difficulties confronted by any small farmer in an era of food-industry, agricultural capitalism. To compete with the large agricultural corporations is difficult if not impossible. To even attempt to enter the same market as these corporate giants, the agriculturalist must invest in huge modern machinery (some balers cost as much as $25,000), vast spreads of land and expensive irrigating equipment, all well out of the reach of most Native American farmers.

Furthermore, the long-lasting effects of the Dawes Act render farming or ranching difficult. The years following that program of individual land allotment saw a good deal of Native American land pass into white hands. What land did remain in Native American ownership has been subdivided by inheritance to a confusing degree. This may leave the individual with small patches of land all over a given reservation. Farming such small chunks of land is extremely impractical and in some cases—say where the individual owns one quarter of an acre—ridiculous. A hypothetical example of what can happen follows: Joe, who lives on a midwestern reservation

14. When whites later found they had missed a trick and that something of value *did* exist on Native American land, they took it back. The classic example of this trend is the case of the Black Hills, which were deemed worthless and included in the Sioux reservation until gold was discovered in them, whereupon the United States changed the treaty to remove the Hills from Sioux ownership.

had a grandfather who received 160 acres by the Dawes Act. The grandfather had four sons, each of them, including Joe's father, inheriting 40 acres. Joe, being one of six children, then becomes owner of 6²/₃ acres. Now Joe also may have become heir to property—from his mother, from a childless uncle, or a brother killed in Korea—in different locations on the reservation. Obviously, to cultivate his holding Joe would have to spend most of his day driving a tractor (if he could afford one) from one little tract to another. This situation is typical of many throughout the reservation system. The result is that the joint heirs to a 160-acre parcel of land usually lease it to a white farmer, and each heir receives a check for his or her portion of the land. There is a problem here, too. While whites can lease property on the free market, the Native American must have approval of the BIA for any land-lease transaction. Essentially this means that the bureau acts as a middleman, setting the rates and dealing with the white leasers, then mailing checks to the Native American. There is, very often, a sweetheart arrangement between the bureau and the local white farmers, whereby the bureau makes Native American lands available at lease rates far below those of other lands in the area. The farmer can then rent cheap and sell his products high, realizing a good profit, while the Native American heirs remain trapped in poverty, depending on the low rent they have been paid. This system is self-perpetuating, as each generation splits the ownership of the original parcel several times. In addition, children are denied the Native American role models they need by seeing whites in control of Native American lands while their own fathers have been rendered unemployed.

With jobs in the white market-place so hard to come by, the question is inevitably raised of the establishment of a Native American job sector—reservation industries owned either by Native Americans or by outside corporations who would employ Native Americans. Several different sets of problems arise in this regard. First, there are facts of life which make it difficult to persuade corporations to establish businesses on reservations. The lack of water and, in some cases, electricity means that the corporation will have to invest a great deal in the physical set-up, bringing in its own power and plumbing systems. The geographical isolation of many reservations renders them inaccessible to markets. Many reservations lack such bare essentials as the paved roads necessary for transportation of raw materials and finished products. Landing strips, and/or decent highways, therefore, also become a part of the investment the corporation is called upon to make. Finally, the corporation which intends to employ a large number of Native Americans must be prepared to invest in a training program.

Even given these demanding criteria, a few corporations have ventured onto the reservations to set up factories, and they have made the improvements necessary for a viable industry. But there have been unfortunate results in such cases. Having obtained tribal council approval for their endeavor, some corporations have followed the old pattern of disregarding promises the Native American believed were made in good faith. For example, most agreements to allow outside industry to settle on the reservation are made with the understanding that the new factory will provide jobs for the many unemployed Native Americans who reside there. When the factory is operating, however, the corporations have proceeded to hire *few* Native Americans. Those hired are often paid substandard wages and relegated to the lowest jobs on the ladder, with little opportunity for advancement. In addition, many traditional Native Americans are wary of outside industries and the effect that they may have on the ecological balance of the reservation. Strip-mining, oil wells, and heavy industry leave environmental destruction in their wake which, some contend, is scarcely worth the slight decline in unemployment that they bring about. Moreover, they simply bring the colonial nature of all Native American life in the United States closer to home, claim the elders. The fact that white industrialists become the controllers of what little land is left in Native American hands offends many Native Americans, who call for self-determination: they would like to see all industry on the reservation in Native American hands, tribally, not individually, owned, employing all Native Americans at high wages, with the profits returning to the people.

Education

Education presents a dismal picture, too, with dropout rates fifty percent higher than the rest of the population. Fewer than eighteen percent of students in federally run Native American schools go on to college. Results of tests indicate that while Native American children perform almost as well as white children on achievement tests that are nonverbal, their verbal work is affected by their lack of English language skills and knowledge of white culture.[15]

The same inconsistency that prevailed in territorial and economic matters has been the rule in education. At first a few schools teaching technical skills were established on or near reservations. Two eastern boarding schools, the Haskell Institute and the Carlisle Indian School, in the latter half of the nineteenth century took Native American children away from home, until outcries against the uprooting of children and separation of families brought about the establishment of schools nearer home. However, because of the distance involved, many of these are also boarding schools. These schools, unfortunately, did not seem to train children for economically successful life, nor did they really prepare the Native American child for higher education by teaching the academic subjects that would permit him or her to go on to college.[16] In all instances, an effort was made to de-Indianize the Native American. Children were sometimes kidnapped from their homes by BIA employees and forced to attend BIA schools.

15. Bruce A. Chadwick, "The Inedible Feast," in Bahr, Chadwick, and Day, *Native Americans Today*, pp. 131-45.

16. See Mead, *Changing Culture*, pp. 113-29, for a description of early education.

Physical punishment, unheard of in most Native American cultures, was and sometimes still is cruelly applied.[17]

Both Parmee, who studied the Apache, and the Waxes, who studied education at Pine Ridge, noted that reservation parents do not take an active interest in their children's education, and they stress the need to make education relevant to the parents as well as to the children. Often, because the values of home and school are so different, the child must choose between being a good Native American and being a good student. The Wax study places more importance on the effect on Native American children of interaction between the two cultures, stressing as they do two different sets of values. In addition, white teachers are considered in their roles as socializers, not as beings who come into the child's life after his personality is completely formed. The parents' exclusion from active involvement with the schools (an example of institutional racism) is presented as a wedge driven between the two worlds in which the child lives. The Waxes urge those coming in contact with Native American children and their families to become sensitized to Native American values and to attempt to make educational programs responsive to the needs of the entire community.[18] Parmee's study of Apache education also points to the incompatibility of school and reservation life, but he bluntly includes the anti-Native American attitudes of white educators in his explanation of the Native American child's passive failure in school.[19]

The Coleman report found that the deficiencies of Native American children in school work were most strongly related to language problems, "cultural deprivation," and negative

17. A description of twentieth-century education is presented by Robert Burnett and John Koster in *The Road to Wounded Knee* (New York: Bantam Books, 1974).

18. Murray Wax and Rosalie Wax, "The Enemies of the People," in Bahr, Chadwick and Day, *Native Americans Today,* pp. 177-92.

19. Edward A. Parmee, *Formal Education and Culture Change: A Modern Apache Community and Government Education Programs* Tucson, Arizona: University of Arizona Press, 1968).

self-concept.[20] Those factors frequently cited as reasons for poor performance—facilities, curriculum, and quality of teachers—were not strongly correlated with the performance of Native American youngsters. This finding is particularly significant if we consider it in the light of a theory of institutional racism. All three of the major variables are related to each other and attributable to institutional racism.

The "language problem," as it is called, reflects the cultural white supremacy and ethnocentric Anglo bias of the educational system: the language problem would not be a problem at all if children were taught in their own language. Language is obviously a major problem for children who, at home, speak something other than standard middle-class English. Native American children who have, until first grade, spoken a tribal language or even "reservation English," find themselves in a classroom where the most basic skills are being conveyed in a language they do not comprehend. Some children literally have no idea what the teacher is saying. To compound the problem, the children are tested on these skills and their performance judged in terms of a national "norm." Small wonder that by such measures they appear to be behind majority-group children.

Incidentally, such tests are very good examples of institutional racism in action. A "correct" answer for test items is based on Anglo culture and the norms that flow from it. Especially on verbal tests, there may be no *intrinsic* correctness to a response but only a correctness as the majority culture defines it. In other words, the performance of white middle-class children establishes the norm for these tests, and the performance of other children is deemed "good" or "bad" depending on the degree to which it conforms to that norm. Thus we can see the arbitrary establishment of an ethnocentric cultural system within the educational institution.

Children who speak a language other than English are not

20. James S. Coleman et al., *Equality of Educational Opportunity* (Washington, D.C.: Government Printing Office, 1966).

alone in suffering from these arrangements. Children who speak an English that is not middle-class suffer as well. The black ghetto child, the reservation Native American, and the working-class white (who says "he don't" or "they was") all may do poorly on verbal tests. The unfortunate aspect of this situation, of course, is that those in the field of education (and many others) do not view correct English simply as conformity to middle-class verbal norms, but tend to equate it with intelligence. Thus children who speak some variant of the language emerge from the testing situation and from interaction with their teachers labeled *stupid*, not just speakers of another kind of English. This link between the speaking of standard English and concepts of intelligence affects both teacher expectations for students and students' feelings about themselves.

Teachers have been observed by many social scientists to be very much attuned to language differences and to show more positive behavior toward students who use standard English.[21] More attention is given to the intellectual and emotional growth of these middle-class children when, for example, compositions are discussed in class. The working-class child's work in this situation is discussed in terms of what grammatical corrections are needed.

Certainly those students who are treated seriously and with respect by their teachers are likely to perform better and to enjoy school more than children who are constantly treated with disapproval. Such children may lose self-esteem and come to view school as an unfriendly place. This is reflected in the high dropout rate among groups of nonstandard English speakers. As long as racial and social class speech patterns influence the expectations and attitudes of teachers, we can safely say that language and the schools will serve to perpetuate the existing class system of the society. Higher education is an important pathway to upward mobility, and the lack of

21. The work of anthropologist Jules Henry is particularly sensitive in this regard.

it confines these children to the same occupational options which were available to their parents, maintaining the status quo for another generation. Thus language may function to lower self-esteem and future expectations on an intraracial level, as well as for minority racial groups, with poor whites being victimized by sanctions against their own "non-normative" speech patterns.

In the case of Native Americans, language has always been recognized by white educators as being of key importance, although, as we have seen, not always for the right reasons. Physical punishment for the speaking of tribal languages characterized almost all of the early schools and is still employed in some schools. There are two reasons for this. The first is the educators' fear of children who could have secrets from them by speaking in a "foreign" tongue. The second reason was the desire to use the schools as deculturating institutions, turning little Native Americans into English-speaking, Christian, Anglo-like citizens, much as the children of the immigrants were being deculturated by the schools in the East.

The introduction of Native American teachers and teacher's aides, and growing community participation in educational matters on the part of many Native American parents, as well as the enlightened establishment of bilingual programs on reservations, have eased the situation somewhat. However, there is a need for more Native American teachers. In the absence of these, some tribal groups are requesting that white teachers be required to demonstrate a knowledge of tribal language and culture before being permitted to teach on the reservation.

The Coleman report cites cultural deprivation as a second major factor in determining the academic achievement of Native American children. "Cultural deprivation," as Chadwick has pointed out in his paper, "The Inedible Feast," would be better phrased as cultural differences.[22] Wax has called the entire notion of cultural deprivation "vacuum" ideology, im-

22. Chadwick, "Inedible Feast."

plying as it does that there is *no* culture in Native American homes.[23] Here we have a perfect example of the Western assessment of those who spring from other cultural backgrounds: they are not different but deprived; their culture is not unusual or interesting, it does not exist. The Coleman report may have told us more about the schools than about the children, for if cultural deprivation, which is really cultural difference, is strongly associated with poor school performance, may it not be precisely because our educational system is predicated upon a familiarity with white culture, that it is mysterious and to an extent irrelevant to those who do not share that familiarity? The Eskimo child confronted by a test in which cows, picket fences, and the ubiquitous Spot figure prominantly is being confronted by a series of symbols which are utterly void of meaning for him.

Considering all of this, it is hardly surprising that poor self-concept figures as the third important variable in the Coleman data. But rather than see these as three separate variables relating to the degree of accomplishment in the school, they would be better viewed as a feedback system.

Most Native American children attend one of three types of schools: BIA-run boarding schools, BIA day schools or public schools which are predominantly white, and religious boarding or day schools.

A great deal has been written about the poor conditions that exist at many BIA boarding schools. Among these conditions are physical punishment, poor housing, inadequate staff-pupil ratios, the ethnocentrism of teachers, the cruelties of half-blood against full-blooded children, and the use of such powerful tranquilizing drugs as thorazine for disciplinary purposes.[24] Christianity has historically and in the present era been stressed over indigenous religion. In short, efforts to destroy Native American culture and make the Native American pupil

23. Murray L. Wax et al., "Formal Education in an American Indian Community." Supplement to *Social Problems* 2, no. 3 (1964).
24. See Burnett and Koster, *Road to Wounded Knee*, pp. 42-70.

ashamed of his or her identity have characterized this system of education. While Havighurst and Fuchs, in their recent comprehensive study of Native American education, dispute the inadequacies of these schools and cast doubt upon some of the horror stories,[25] testimony from adult Native Americans makes it clear that attendance at such schools was very often an unhappy and frightening experience for children. This is especially true when very small children are removed from their families and transported such distances to school that it is impossible for their parents to visit them.

The BIA day schools are also staffed by BIA personnel and thus fall prey to many of the same problems as the boarding schools, ethnocentrism and shaming in particular. Burnett states that teachers in the Navajo schools have been observed using the children's own culture as a disciplinary threat:[26] for example, "All right, go ahead and talk while we're working, if you want to spend the rest of your life living in some old hogan!" Although the BIA offers an optional course on Native American cultures for its teachers, few avail themselves of the opportunity to learn about the societies in which their students spend their daily lives. Also, since having textbooks like the rest of the society is regarded as a step forward (better than out-of-date texts), these children are being exposed to the same colorful but unfair image of their own people as white children. History as it is taught in these schools is history from the white perspective. Custer is a national hero, his opponents are "savages."[27] It is difficult to involve parents in the activities of the schools: their own experiences with white education have been either minimal or of the boarding-school variety, and they are alienated from the schools.

Native American children who attend the white day schools have become political pawns. Under the Johnson-O'Malley

25. Estelle Fuchs and Robert Havighurst, *To Live on this Earth*, (Garden City, N.Y.: Doubleday, 1972).

26. Burnett and Koster, *Road to Wounded Knee*, pp. 42-70.

27. One hundred years from now, will Vietnamese children be taught that Lieutenant Calley was a hero?

Act, public schools in which Native American children are enrolled may receive payments from the BIA for every Native American child in the school. Thus even very racist schools attempt to raise their Native American enrollment, because these pupils bring in more money. While the Johnson-O'Malley Act was intended to improve the quality of Native American education through the application of these funds to remedial language programs and others of special help to Native American youngsters, there has been flagrant violation of this intent. Schools use Johnson-O'Malley funds for many purposes: new football fields or pianos, for example, which Native American children never use. Only recently has legislation been proposed which would give tribal groups control over their own Johnson-O'Malley funds. If the funds were being ill used, under this new act the tribe could refuse to continue funding and could remove its youngsters from the school.

Getting an education is difficult for the Native American youngster. He or she must contend with the conditions described above or more. Merely getting to school may be difficult. Some Native American children must rise at five o'clock in the morning, walk several miles to the schoolbus stop, then ride for fifty miles over unpaved and bumpy roads to get to school. In the evening they must repeat this process in reverse. Many are ashamed of their inadequate or "un-cool" clothing. This poverty-related problem is compounded by the difficulties of keeping neat and clean in a situation where there is no water except what is brought from miles away in buckets every day. Poor health, to be discussed in further detail below, may raise the rate of absenteeism, and a child who is already having academic problems because of the language difference may fall even further behind because of illness.

Given all the cultural and social-structural obstacles to getting an education, the amazing aspect of Native American life may not be that the dropout rate is so high, but that not everyone drops out. Those who push on to high school, despite all the hurdles, meet with more problems at that level. Dating begins then, and for Native Americans in white schools many racial slurs may occur in this context. Also these students may be labeled "disciplinary problems" if they try to stand up for their rights or refuse to "play the Indian role"—quiet and stoic. At this level of the educational system, the Native American student begins to meet persons who have accepted the cultural stereotype of the nonscholastic Native American. These people refuse to believe that he or she is capable of good work, even when presented with evidence to the contrary. Prejudice emerges as the embarrassed white flounders about for an explanation of the behavior which contradicts his image of what Native American students are like. Thus, one highly intelligent woman who was, when I knew her, a promising prelaw student at an Ivy League university, recalled that during her high-school years, she was accused of cheating every time she did well on a test or homework assignment.

This tendency also emerges in the advice guidance counselors give Native American youngsters. One prominent Native American leader recalls that when he asked about college, his high-school advisor laughed at him. The idea of a Native American wishing to go to college struck him as singularly amusing.

Thus, few do go on. Many who do become overwhelmed or angered by university life and return home, but increasing numbers are going through college, and some go on to graduate and professional schools. Interestingly, because so many Native American problems are rooted in law and in treaties, a large number of Native Americans who have gone on to graduate work have elected to study law.

Health

The health conditions on most reservations are poor. Many Native Americans die in the first years of life, and the life expectancy for the group is lower than that for whites. Special health problems arise out of the impoverished conditions which have left this segment of the population unserved by electricity, indoor plumbing, clean water and decent, well-heated housing. Flies and other pests spread infection and keep diseases long vanished from the general population alive in Native American groups. For example, bubonic plague is listed as a cause of several deaths among the Native American population during the past decade.

Two sets of morbidities seem to be the primary agents of ill health among Native Americans, now that contagious diseases have been fairly well controlled by inoculations and antibiotics. These are (1) poverty-caused ailments and (2) tension- and stress-related problems.

Poverty-related diseases arise out of lack of sanitation. Gastrointestinal problems are prominent in this regard. The flies and the lack of refrigeration cause contamination of food with predictable ill effects. Poor ventilation, lack of heat, and overcrowding cause severe respiratory problems. The distance between home and medical facilities, complicated by poor and unpaved roads, may mean that severe lacerations go untreated. This can leave permanent scarring in some cases and can lead to fatality from infection or tetanus in others.

Stress-related diseases such as ulcers, heart trouble, and hypertension have risen in the past two decades in the Native American population. Alcoholism is a major problem in many locations. The suicide rate is very high, especially among young people, and accidents are a primary cause of death.

In health-care as in the other institutions, most of the important people are white, and there are very few Native American physicians, dentists or other medical personnel. Some programs have been mounted to improve this situation, but it is highly unlikely that Native American children today will find one of their own people in a position of authority in a health-care center. Whites who do not understand the culture may behave rudely or inconsiderately to Native American patients, or misinterpret their behavior, which can make the people reluctant to utilize the health services that do exist.

Health care for urban Native Americans is a problem, as it is unclear what agencies are responsible for them. Most town medical centers or hospitals are not aware that the BIA will assume responsibility for urban dwellers, and send them away. Only if a person is a veteran can he be assured of treatment in a city, if there is a Veterans' Administration installation.

The reservation installations are often out of date, poorly budgeted and understaffed. This is a problem of increasing seriousness with the ending of the draft. For many young physicians, the Public Health Service alternative to life in the armed forces, especially in Vietnam, seemed a good choice. No longer threatened with Vietnam, fewer physicians are going into Public Health Service, the agency responsible for Native American medical care. Testimony in Congressional hearings on Native American health indicates that in several years there may not be enough staff to run the health facilities. Thus what gains have been made in the area of controlling childhood diseases and in the use of surgery may be set back several decades, unless persons can be found willing to administer to the Native Americans.

Urbanism

Urbanism is rapidly becoming an important factor in the life of the Native American. Begun under a 1954 BIA policy, "relocation," as it is called, has brought increasing numbers of Native Americans to such centers as San Francisco, Los Angeles, Phoenix and Denver. Other Native American families are "self-relocated" and have gravitated to these centers, as well as to New York and Chicago, on their own, without BIA help. It is estimated that the Native American population of New York City has increased from 4,366 in 1960 to over 10,000 in 1970.[28]

Usually the incentive to relocate is economic. Jobs are not available on or near most reservations, and discrimination against Native Americans seems to be stronger in towns near reservations, making it difficult for Native Americans to find

---

28. See Howard M. Bahr, "An End to Invisibility," in Bahr, Chadwick, and Day, *Native Americans Today*, pp. 404-12.

a job near home. The move to a large urban area, where civil rights are more assured, appeals to many Native Americans. During the period of "termination," the ultimate goal of Native American policy was total assimilation of the Native American population within the greater society, and most education programs were geared to this end. As described above, native language and customs have always been discouraged by BIA schools. To this deculturating program was added job training in skills which could be applied only off the reservation. A person whose training was in furniture upholstery, for example, had little choice but to relocate, as he could not do a profitable business on the reservation where most homes are furnished with orange crates and wooden furniture.

The urban Native American has only recently become the object of sociological inquiry so there is little data on him. However, what studies exist show him to be younger and slightly better educated than the Native American population at large. Some have had experience and contact with whites during military service. Most urban Native Americans report that while they maintain friendly relations with people they meet at work, their real affection and moments of social intimacy are reserved for fellow Native Americans. They look to the reservation with nostalgia, and most state that if jobs and economic security were available there, they would return home.[29]

Native American organizations have grown in urban centers, usually manned by a core of activists, and these centers attract Native Americans for sports events, dances or pow-wows.

Some Native Americans do not remain in the cities. The disorientation they experience in their initial days of urban life may bring forth or exaggerate unhappiness and anomie. Loneliness, drinking, and family quarrels may result, so that a return to the reservation seems the only safe course.[30] Later

29. Ibid.
30. T. O. Graves, "The Personal Adjustments of Navajo Indian Migrants to Denver," in Bahr, Chadwick, and Day, *Native Americans Today*, pp. 444-66.

on these same people may try city life again. A Lincoln, Nebraska study of urban Omahas found that there was a great deal of mobility back and forth between the reservation and town, and Graves notes the same pattern among the Navajo.[31]

Most researchers agree that one result of urbanization has been an increased feeling of Native American unity. Ablon notes that for some Native Americans the full realization of their Native American identity comes with the move to town, where their physical features and customs are so distinctive that they become conscious of them. Also, Native Americans do not seem to cluster in neighborhoods as past migrants in the cities have done. They meet other Native Americans through work, BIA office meetings, and the Native American centers, and their acquaintances are not necessarily of the same tribe as themselves. In the loneliness of the city, one is overjoyed to see another Native American, whatever his or her tribal affiliation, and old rivalries are forgotten in the face of a new pan-Native Americanism. The Native American organizations also encourage intertribal friendship through a sharing of songs, costumes, and dances.[32] This has had a unifying effect on the Native American population and has nurtured the growth of Red Power.

The city can bring decided advantages to adults—good jobs, better housing, sanitation, and good education. In addition, adults can offset the culture shock of city life through friendships with other Native Americans, informal socializing, and participation in activities at the urban Native American centers. Unfortunately, children do not have such cushions against the blows of urban life. They must go to school, where they find themselves a small minority, the objects of prejudice on the part of teachers and other children.

31. Margot Liberty, "The Urban Reservation" (Ph.D. diss., University of Minnesota, 1973); and Graves, "Personal Adjustments."

32. Joan Ablon, "Relocated American Indians in the San Francisco Bay Area: Social Interaction and Indian Identity," *Human Organization* 23 (1964): 296-304.

Red Power

Until 1960, the Native Americans seemed a passive and powerless group. The policy of termination was still in effect, despite the outraged cries of anthropologists and older Native American leaders. The decade since then has witnessed change in the political outlook of Native American groups.

The symbolic act of taking over Alcatraz and the fish-ins in the state of Washington heralded a new self-assertive era. The National Indian Chicago Conference, meeting in 1961, declared: "We, the majority of the Indian people of the United States of America . . . have the inherent right of self-government." The conference also came out strongly against termination and expressed the desire that their lands remain intact and under government protection.

Native Americans have taken active measures to prevent the further loss of land, taken over deserted government property, staged demonstrations at the BIA in Washington, D.C., and occupied the village of Wounded Knee. While Red Power has appealed primarily to the young, urban, more highly educated Native American, its appeal has been far-reaching.

What social forces have brought about such a surge of activity in this previously quiescent minority? What have been its effects on the population, both white and Native American? Three Native American organizations have been instrumental in organizing the diverse tribes for unified action: the National Indian Youth Council, a group of younger Native Americans; the National Congress of American Indians, composed of older members, with goals viewed by the younger group as limited; and the American Indian Movement (AIM), which draws members from urban and reservation centers and appeals mainly to the young, although it has support from older persons, too. The traditional respect of Native American youth for elders has made it possible for people to work together in many instances, despite their differences, which include a debate over political tactics and disagreement over the need for continuation of the BIA.

Termination was probably the trigger of the Red Power movement. As whole tribes were put out of existence, and the mineral and game rights of others were threatened, Native Americans began to realize that this might be their last chance to hold on to their land and their identity. This policy, combined with the extreme poverty in which most Native Americans live, created a determination to bring about change. At the same time an increased awareness of the life-styles of other Americans brought about a sense of relative deprivation.

World War II, and the Korean and Vietnam wars produced the Native American veteran, a man who had been exposed to new ideas and cross-cultural situations. This new Native American was also aware of the emerging Third World countries, which based their claims to independence on their original ownership of land colonized by whites, and the obvious parallels were not lost on him. Many of these veterans became college students under the G.I. Bill and were exposed to even more political ideas. Education in turn led to the creation of a small middle class with political awareness, and the time and skills for political organization and activity.

The black Civil Rights movement was undoubtedly an influence on the Native Americans, setting precedents of legal appeal and civil disobedience in the effort to attain equality. Some of the younger Native American leaders, such as Clyde Warrior, were involved in the early voter registration drives in Mississippi. But, by and large, the effects of the black movement on Native Americans have been indirect, creating a state of relative deprivation as well as the anticipation of change.

Recent advances in communications, particularly the mass media, also made Native Americans aware of the rise of nonwhite peoples around the world with demands for equality and self-government. Television antennae are not an infrequent sight on reservations, and transistor radios abound.

Urbanization, too, contributed to Native American unity and acquainted Native Americans with methods of lobbying and gaining attention for their cause. The better standard of living in the cities, especially in the area of health, made Native Americans further aware of how badly off their people were as a group. Newly aware of the perils of dealing with a more legally knowledgeable white society, such tribes as the Navajo have engaged the services of white lawyers to protect their rights, and have launched a program to educate several Native lawyers in the next few years.

In addition, strong and articulate leaders helped crystallize this movement. Vine Deloria, whose polished wit is in part the product of elite eastern schools, seaman Mad Bear Anderson, with his gift for the humorous exposé of white foolishness, and Vernon Bellecourt, with his political sophistication and burning anger, have all drawn their people together with a new optimism and have attracted sympathetic white attention.

The demonstration elementary school at Rough Rock backed by the Ford Foundation and the Navajo nation, which has been the focus of much attention, predicates its entire approach to education on Native American pride and self-determination.

Tribes taking part in this study

A brief overview of the societies in which the children in this study live will illustrate a number of the trends noted above. One condition of access to the Native American sample was that the names of individuals and tribal groups would not be used in the manuscript, a stipulation to which I gladly adhere. Therefore, in the descriptions which follow, the tribal groups will be referred to as Group 1, Group 2, and Group 3.

Group 1

This southwestern group of Native Americans have lived along the banks of the Gila River, south of Phoenix, Arizona, for all historical times. They are believed to be descendants of the Hohokam people who built vast irrigation systems in that part of the world.[33]

Agriculture provided the basis of subsistence and was done by the men of the tribe, with some assistance from the women. Fields were irrigated by a sophisticated system of canals, the ruins of which can be seen today. Crops were abundant. Trade took place with the closely related Papago tribe; agricultural produce was traded by the tribe to the Papago for desert products like cactus fruit. Hunting of small animals and fishing added protein to the otherwise all-vegetable diet.

Politically the group adhered to a policy of discussion and unanimous agreement in decision making. Often it took some time to make decisions, as one can well imagine, but the insistence on total consensus insured that once a decision was made or a policy formulated, it would have universal support.

A peaceful people, they went to war to defend rather than conquer. They were good warriors, but did not remain long in battle, as religion demanded that a warrior mourn his victim for sixteen days, as he would a departed kinsman. The group never engaged in battle against white settlers, and early notes of wagon masters and military describe them as a friendly and helpful people. White ways of dress and the English language were adopted readily.

Although many members had been converted to Catholicism in the sixteenth century by a wandering Spanish priest, at the end of the last century a Presbyterian missionary was sent to serve as a schoolteacher and to convert the people to his faith. Thus about half the present inhabitants of the reservation are Catholic and half Protestant.

The tribe was left alone, except for passing wagon trains bound for California, until the late nineteenth century. However, when whites became interested in the Phoenix area as a health and ranching area, the pattern of buying land from native tribesmen and channeling off their precious water supply asserted itself. Land developers have utilized the water

33. Historical and demographic material in this section is based on the work of Underhill and Russell.

which the group depended upon for their agriculture. Now, strangers to the area have little need of the sign which informs them that they are entering the reservation, for the green of irrigated fields abruptly gives way to desert as the boundary is crossed. Poverty prevails, unemployment is high, and farming is impossible for most, because of the water situation. Recently, however, improved communication with other tribes, especially the vanguard Navajo, has alerted them to the advantages of legal assistance and utilization of available government funds for improving their economic conditions.

There is a large Model Cities program on the reservation, and an industrial park is being constructed and will be shared with the Papago. People are being trained in nursing, agriculture and IBM key-punching and programming, which, if used at the industrial park, would make it possible for the people to solve their employment problem without relocating. How many Native Americans the park will employ is unknown. Day-care centers have been initiated so that young couples can both train for jobs and obtain them. Children in these centers are fed two meals; the lunch meat provides perhaps the only meat in their diet, which is usually heavy with fry bread and beans. The children also play games, are exposed to a variety of toys, and are taught elementary health measures.

Many of the low-level administrative positions in the Model Cities program are held by Native Americans, and the day-care centers are Native American-staffed. An effort is being made to educate Native American women at Arizona State University to qualify for certification, so that more Native Americans will be teaching in the elementary and high schools. However, at the time of my research, the only Native American women in the schools were aides. The head teachers were white.

Despite the proximity of the Phoenix area, with its several medical facilities, and the presence of a public-health facility on the reservation itself, there is still much evidence of poor health. The types of morbidity which are evident are poverty-related. With the absence of agriculture, the people have come to rely on foods imported to the reservation, especially those high in carbohydrates. The result is a great deal of obesity, hypertension, and the highest diabetes rate of any group in the United States.

Water has been limited to schools, government buildings, and missions. It may be piped to some residences in the future. A very clean people, they may make ten car-trips to town every evening to bring in enough water for children to bathe. (One can imagine, too, the fire hazards inherent in the combination of no water, gas lanterns, and the Arizona heat.) The absence of water and of sanitary facilities causes unhealthful conditions within the homes. Gastroenteritis and other diseases of the gastrointestinal tract are quite common. Trachoma, a dangerous eye infection, is also common and can spread easily when many family members must share bathing water.

Housing is still of the dirt- and log-cabin variety, with no heat and poor ventilation. The result is respiratory trouble: many of the children I interviewed had runny noses, coughs, and such chest congestion that their breathing could be heard across a classroom.

Accidents occur frequently and may go untreated. Many children come to school with recent injuries; lacerations and burns are particularly common.

Interviews with parents reveal that they worry about the children's education and seem to place a high value on it as a means to better economic status. However, the parents' own unhappy school experiences, the lack of communication between school and parent, and ill health of children and adults all militate against progress in this area, and both parents and educators mention dropping out as a major problem.

There is, however, something of a cultural renaissance here, and it is hoped that its incorporation into education will keep children in school and interested. People recently awakened to the fact that their language, crafts, and dances were dying out. A large art center has been built where they and neighboring tribes bring paintings and handmade items for sale, and young people are learning the old techniques. There is some interest in finding an older person to provide instruction in the tribal language at the center. Children have been taught the traditional dances, and the Head Start class from one school became quite well known for their dancing in costumes made by older women of the tribe.

There is a small but extremely active middle class of judges, government employees and teachers, who are involved on all levels of community life, from legal battles for water to Boy Scout hikes. This group provides leadership in innovation which might intimidate other tribal members. However, there is a good deal of factionalism. The wordy, bureaucratic tendencies of government programs and their white advisors conflict with traditional Native American ways of reaching decisions.

Despite their English language, rock-and-roll records, and miniskirts, the adults are distinctly Native American and have a strong sense of belonging to a group which is labeled "Indian." This is revealed in almost every conversation one has with them, as their speech is liberally punctuated with such phrases as "our Indian ways," "out here in Indian country," and "our Indian people." There is little desire to join the white man's world (to do so might be to take on his "crazy" hurried ways and neuroses), but only to acquire some of the advantages he has that make life a little easier. Intermarriage is not envied. White marriage-partners are rarely spoken of by name, even after many years of marriage; they are referred to, for instance, as "that white man who married Delores." The dissolution of such unions is usually an occasion for great celebration.

On the whole, then, the group has a history of agriculture and peaceful coexistence with others. Both of these traits, however, have been weakened by whites, who have victimized them and caused them to reexamine their friendliness. Poverty is the rule. It remains to be seen whether government efforts to upgrade the skills of the population for contemporary job markets will bear fruit.

Group 2

The second Native American group studied was a northeastern-Nebraska, upper-Missouri tribe who have always maintained friendly relations with whites.[34] Of the same language family as the Plains warriors, they nonetheless differ from other Plains groups in culture and economy. Agriculture was practiced by the women of the tribe and added to the hunters' usual meat diet. Hunting, the male pursuit, was given all the importance in ritual and legend, and agriculture was devalued. However, it is probable that agriculture provided the bulk of the diet, as the group was only seminomadic, engaging in one large buffalo-hunt every year.

There was a complex system of exogenous clans, and a further division of the tribe into moieties of Earth and Sky people. Wealth and power were not distributed in this society as equally as they were in Group 1. Tribal council members made decisions for the group. In addition, the members of the doctoring societies had claim to more prestige than other members of the group. Access to membership in these societies was quite limited. Since the members were paid for their services in goods, they began to accumulate more property than nonmembers and thus were in a better position to gain social roles which involved contributions of wealth: for example, because they could pay high bride-prices, they could marry into powerful families. Thus, the beginning of a system of social stratification existed in this society, perhaps even before contact with whites took place.

After the establishment of the reservation, people continued to engage in farming, and a fairly good adjustment was made to the new life, at least by the women, who were doing what they had been doing for generations. Men, however, were without socially viable roles after the disappearance of large game animals and their confinement to the reservation. The

34. Background material on Group 2 draws on the work of Dorsey, Fortune, and Mead.

government encouraged the building of frame houses and the acquisition of canning and sewing skills on the part of the women. The passage of the Dawes Act gave each Native American a parcel of land and brought speculators to this rich country. Many Native Americans sold their land for a fast profit, which they soon spent. The rich, rolling fields of ripening corn that impress the visitor to the reservation are deceptive, as most of them are now owned by or leased to whites.

Family quarrels are frequent, and drinking bouts common. Many men cannot find employment and thus may feel impotent to improve the destiny of their often large families. This type of man is the prime protagonist in drinking and fighting episodes, although females are not blameless. One child told me sadly, "My grandma got arrested again last night. She wanted to get into the new jail [a local novelty], but they put her in the old one. Now she's ashamed cuz the judge is her son and she got to come up before him." Children are especially bewildered by these drinking episodes, when usually fond and permissive elders become unlike themselves and act in unpredictable ways. One teenager told me that she puts all the other children in the car on nights when the parents drink and drives around the reservation until daylight so that she and her brothers and sisters will not come to physical harm.

There is a clinic in the village, and it is used. The children seemed to be less beset by obvious physical ailments than the children of the other tribes studied. This is probably due to a certain degree of sophistication on the part of parents, who may have learned about health care during periods of urban residence, and to the fact that the reservation is small enough for people to have easy access to the facilities that do exist. The Public Health nurse, who works on the reservation, is also well liked.

The need for jobs has taken many to nearby urban centers. There are growing Native American populations in Lincoln, Omaha, and Sioux Falls. There is a good deal of visiting back and forth between town and reservation, and occasions of tribal importance such as funerals and powwows attract tribesmen from great distances. There is also much actual moving back and forth between the two places. Many of the reservation people have had some experience with urban life, and most of the urban people were raised on the reservation. There are, however, a few second-generation urban dwellers who are very well adapted to city life, know how to cope with bureaucracies, and are prospering. A group in Lincoln now own their own business and are doing quite well. Their adaptation to the city has not interfered with their sense of Native American identity, however. Several organizations have been established in Lincoln, and they attract a wide membership and sponsor powwows and dances. They also are a source of help to newly arrived Native Americans from the reservation.

On the whole, the people of this group seem more at ease with whites and are more ready to befriend them than the other tribes studied. It appears that they have internalized white values more than the others, but this may be only appearance. We have already noted the class structure of traditional society, and the socially approved accumulation of property. Perhaps these aspects of their own culture have allowed these Native Americans to accept white values more easily than the other tribes.

Politically, the urban dwellers are rather active and were quick to recognize the success of the black movement and to lobby for equal rights and opportunities. However, there have been few financial sources of support for them. They lack tribal funds and have received little help from government or other sources. The reservation seems to be taking little advantage of government programs, and this may also be connected to the existence of a class structure. The present reservation leadership is composed of old, land-holding families who did not sell out after the passage of the Dawes Act, and it is possible that they have a vested interest in maintaining the status quo. In any event, innovation is not encouraged.

Here, too, school seems alienating to the older children, and the dropout rate is high. However, quite a few adults have returned to school and are pursuing degrees.

Group 3

The third tribe studied was the Native American tribe as it exists in American folklore—war-bonneted, pony-riding warriors.[35] Perhaps the best-known Native Americans, Group 3 were nomadic hunters and gatherers who roamed the Great Plains and sloping hills of the Dakotas and lower Wyoming in search of the buffalo. It is believed that they were not always located in this section of the United States, and their legends support the idea that they migrated from east of the Missouri River. The horse, which supplanted the dog as pack animal, helped immeasurably in the adaptation to life on the plains. People could move faster, hunt larger game, and carry heavier loads with the help of the horse; later white weapons also made it easier to hunt and to put down rivals. There was no agriculture to speak of, and cultivated foods were not staples, though the people regarded some crops as delicacies and traded meats and skins for them with more sedentary tribes.

While relations with the rugged French and American traders, whose life-style was not very different from their own, were amicable, the coming of land settlers and those who sought the gold in the Black Hills marked the beginning of hostile relations with whites. The tribe had fought to obtain their territory, and they fought to maintain it against great odds. The fighting skills of the warriors are legendary, symbolized by the battle of the Little Big Horn. However, the Native Americans were up against a force which greatly outnumbered them. Their leader sought sanctuary in Canada, and the rest of the tribe, group by group, came to accept the reservation. White diseases took a huge toll. The people were decimated by disease and demoralized by the loss of their old way of life.

At first no economic system existed to fill the void created by the loss of the buffalo and the establishment of the reservation system. The group was supported by government ra-

35. Material on Group 3 can be found in the writings of Driver, Macgregor, and Erikson.

tions of flour, beef, and other basic foods. However, by the first decade of this century, a cattle-raising economy was soundly established, and the fine horsemen of the tribe had found a way to lead a "man's life" and please the white man at the same time: please some of the white men, that is, for there were others—wealthy cattlemen of the Midwest—who viewed the thriving herds of the Native Americans with alarm, as rivals in the marketplace. By the beginning of the first World War, these interests had succeeded in placing pressure on the government to put a halt to the Native American cattle business, and they were forced to sell their herds.

Since then, there has been no strong economic role for men to play in the society. A few cattle still are owned, and some farming is done, but neither the land nor the climate is very good for cultivation. Some seek work in nearby towns, but most can find only seasonal and unskilled work. Drinking and family dissolution are sometimes the result. Health conditions are poor, despite the presence of a government hospital in the largest reservation town. Homes are the least adequate of any we saw during the research. People live in hollowed-out buses and shacks, some with no windows. This is especially appalling when we consider the South Dakota climate, with its fierce dust and snow storms. There is a good deal of respiratory trouble among the children, and the diets of many are inadequate.

There is a middle class of government employees, church-related employees, and teachers, most of whom live in a government complex and who seem to associate more with one another and with whites of their social class than with the Native Americans in the rural parts of the reservation. Most of these people have adopted white ways and attitudes toward their own people. Some parents feel that these white-oriented tribesmen are the toughest teachers and severest critics they must face. Their attitude is one of disdain and superiority, and there seems to be an effort to show the white reference group how different one is from "other Indians."

In contrast to this group, a new, younger leadership, more attuned to the larger community, has begun to assert itself. It is here that the American Indian Movement has had its strongest impact, first in the occupation of a reservation hamlet and later in Russell Means's campaign for tribal chairmanship.

One of the programs introduced by this more active group has been the new bilingual program at the day school, funded by a Title VII grant. The program went into effect in September 1971, and during our stay with the tribe the staff was engaged in innovative work in the preparation of materials such as textbooks and flash cards in the tribal language. Modeled on the Rough Rock demonstration school, the new program seeks to increase the child's desire to learn by making the school a nonalien environment. It is believed that many of the learning problems faced by the children are really language problems, as they speak a "reservation English." (While almost all adults and children can speak English, many speak Indian in their homes.) In addition, language is used as a symbol of cultural identity in the program. The amount of English used will be increased as the child moves up the academic ladder. The ultimate goal is to produce a graduate who can choose which world he wants to live in. If he elects to remain with his own people, he can do so as an educated person with a skill to contribute to the community, rather than stay by default, as is now often the case. If he wants to find employment in larger cities, he will have the language skills and the education to find a good job.

Obviously, for the program to succeed, changes are needed in other areas of the lives of the people. It will do no good to produce an educated group who want to live on the reservation if there are no jobs to be had there. In the early sixties, a Native American construction company seemed one step in this direction, but it was liquidated when a new tribal chairman took office who preferred that new-housing funds be put into purchased mobile homes, rather than constructed housing. There are more unemployed persons than there are positions available, and greater progress must be made in this area if the education program is really to bear fruit.

It is interesting to note that there is a good deal of skepticism about the program on the part of many of the less educated parents. Having spent all their school years hearing that white ways are the only ways and being punished for speaking their own tongue, they are fearful of having their children in a school where it is the language of instruction. It is necessary to reassure these people that their children will be learning correct English, but they do not easily see the relationship between pride in "Indianness" and academic improvement. This may be because of the greater contact with whites in Dakota country than in Navajo country, which gave birth to the bilingual approach. There, parents welcomed the Native American approach to education and have taken an active interest in the schools. Perhaps as the idea of Native American nationalism spreads among the more isolated people, they will better understand the rationale of the program, but now many are perplexed by it.

Group 3's reservation is larger than either of the other two, and distances between districts are greater; for some parts of the year it is very difficult to get from one to another. There is a good deal of political rivalry between factions of the tribe, so leadership and activity are dispersed rather than central- ized as on the other two reservations. Also, there are many white farmers on the reservation and many whites in positions of authority in the schools, BIA, and the hospital; this has probably tended to undermine Native American leadership. Changes are appearing with the new active leaders, but older people still tend to look to whites for leadership.

In summary, Group 3 is the most economically deprived group in our sample. The rigors of the climate and economic stagnation have left people skeptical of innovation and doubt- ful of their own potential. This has been augmented in the past by the attitude of white and middle-class Native American teachers toward their charges. The loss of the cattle economy has left men without socially valued employment, and this has had unfortunate effects on health and family life. Innovative programs instituted by a young, "Indian Power"-oriented leadership seeks to restore the Native American community as the reference group, a position now occupied to a con- siderable extent by the greater white society.

Thus, the children in this study (with the exception of the urban children) are typical of the reservation child in America. Most live in inadequate housing—shacks, log cabins, even abandoned vehicles such as cars or buses. Less than half of them have electricity in their homes. Few have running water or indoor sanitary facilities. Heating is often by open fire or wood-burning stove, and ventilation may be poor. This situation is difficult enough in the Southwest, where the desert becomes quite cold on winter nights, but as I sat in South Dakota homes with paneless windows, through which the July flies came and went at will, I thought of the harsh plains winters, with their fierce winds and banks of snow, and wondered how these people managed to find warmth in those subzero conditions.

Many of the children are poorly clothed. Almost none of the reservation children wear shoes. Their T-shirts and shorts are often torn and ragged. The beauty of these children is marred by open sores in some cases and the scars of untreated lacerations in others. There are many runny noses and persistent coughs, and a few children I met were severely asthmatic. The lack of health-care facilities, and the distrust that many parents feel for the impersonal and/or rude reception they receive at these facilities, have made it difficult to maintain the health of the children. Often accidents occur, and the combination of poor weather and road conditions (most roads on reservations are not paved) makes it impossible to obtain medical treatment.

A few children look fine—the children of tribal bigwigs, officials, BIA workers, and other government employees. Like white, middle-class children, these youngsters live in modern, government-built and funded split-level housing, see a doctor when they become ill, and go shopping in modern department stores for their school wardrobes. They may have shiny bicycles to ride around the government compound. But they are the exception, and they stand out. It is a sad but not unusual sight to see a ragged little girl circling one of these affluent children, cautiously, admiringly fingering the hem of the Dacron finery, or to see a boy running his hand longingly over the seat of a classmate's new bike.

The schools are basically white-controlled. There are varying degrees of community involvement, the Dakota plains group being the most active of the groups studied in this respect. In most cases, the chain of command can be traced back to a white individual or to white financial control. Thus, in the one community-controlled school that we sampled, the Head Start teacher was white, and the school was dependent on whites for continued financing through a grant.

The "teacher's aide" concept was being widely used in all three communities at the time of the study. This really meant that the classrooms had a white head teacher and numerous Native American aides whom she commanded. (In the urban schools, the teachers were predominantly white, although one school had several black teachers; there was only one Native American aide.) Small children tend to idolize their teachers, and on the reservation, the adulation of the children, especially the girls, for their glamorous young white teachers was quite evident. Children took great interest in the teachers' appearance and clothing, and frequently commented, "You're pretty, Teacher." In the case of the two blond teachers whose classes I observed, I noticed that when the teacher and children were spending a quiet time together, reading a story or singing, a few children would silently move to her side and begin to play with her hair.

When school is not in session, children of six and older play in large independent groups of peers who roam about unsupervised for a large part of the day, returning home quite late in the evenings. Younger children, however, usually stay closer to home under the watchful eye of mother or grandmother, or perhaps an older sibling. There are always many little children around, so that one is never lonely and always has someone with whom to play. Older children assume a good deal of responsibility for smaller ones, and, although they may occasionally tease them, are very protective.

Children are rarely excluded from any community event, as they are considered a most important part of that community. Powwows, hand games, and funerals alike are events in which the children assume their places as members of the group. During the summer, especially, it is a rare week which is without some sort of celebration or religious ceremony. Thus, the life of the reservation child is rich in those communal events which bring together his people in a reaffirmation of their cultural belongingness.

But the reservation children are not completely isolated from the larger society. Saturdays usually see everyone piling into a pickup or car for a marketing trip to some local border town (that is, a town near a reservation). White nurses, doctors, and teachers have invaded the Native American world as well. Many of them live on the reservation, albeit in posh and separate facilities. White welfare workers also become known to many Native American children. Television, in the schools or in the homes of those few affluent government employees, acts like a magnet on the young and provides yet another window on the larger society. One can only imagine what thoughts may occur to the young inhabitant of an abandoned schoolbus as he observes the quaint goings-on of the "Brady Bunch" in their suburban opulence.

This summary chapter has presented an overview of the life conditions of many contemporary Native Americans. The problems of poverty, unemployment, and discrimination have been noted, and the difficulties involved in educational achievement, housing, and health described. The children who took part in this study, it is noted, inhabit the social world which has been staked out for them by the above mentioned circumstances. Although urban children fare somewhat better, most of the children in this sample are poor, inadequately housed and nourished, and do not receive the medical attention that most of our citizens take for granted. Their condition stands in marked contrast to that of the whites, who, because of occupational pursuit or tourists' curiosity, enter the world of the Native American child.

We thus arrive at the conclusion that the world in which the Native American child lives is characterized by institutional racism and its influence on social life.

CHAPTER 3

Racial Attitudes of
Native American Children

———◆◆◆———

Research was carried out during the summer and fall of 1971 with preschool children from the southwestern and midwestern United States. Two hundred and twenty-nine children took part in the study. These included 55 children from a reservation southeast of Phoenix, Arizona; 21 urban members of a Nebraska tribe; 21 from the tribal reserve in the northern part of the state; and 20 Dakota children. The white control group included 43 midwestern children from Lincoln, Nebraska, and 52 southwestern children from Phoenix, Arizona.

Because of the still uncertain meaning of the term "acculturation," we did not wish to add to the already complicated nature of our analysis by including use of the English language or modern dress as an independent variable, but preferred to hold it constant. Therefore, all the groups interviewed are similar in this respect. They all speak English as well as their tribal language and, in most cases, wear modern dress except on religious or other ceremonial occasions. This does not mean that a consideration of this aspect of Indian life is unimportant—indeed, I hope that future research will focus on it. I only note that such consideration was deliberately *not* undertaken in this study, because I elected to focus on the effect of other variables—age, residence, geographical location, and parental activism. I also believe that inclusion of "acculturation" would be unreliable until a more structured and unambiguous concept is defined by that term which could lend itself to analysis. At this point one cannot speak with any real authority about "degrees of acculturation." Of course, randomizing the sampling of tribes would have made it impossible to maintain control of the observation of key variables. Therefore, selective sampling of tribes was used, which allowed us to select groups with respect to the variables in which we were interested. Where more than one tribe filled these requirements, ease of access determined the selection. Limited time and budget also made this method of selection more attractive.

Within the group selected, an intensive effort was made to test the entire population of children between the ages of three and five. Thus, all of the children enrolled in Arizona Model Cities schools, Head Start, day care or nursery schools, are included in the study.[1] Schools were revisited several times to pick up children who might have been absent on the interviewer's previous visit. Testing was also carried out in the summer of 1971 and again in November 1971, to be sure that the summer enrollment had not been biased by the absence of those children who remained at home when older brothers and sisters were out of school to take care of them.

The urban Nebraska sample represents all the Nebraska tribal children between the ages of three and five living in

1. One child, who appeared quite slow and possibly retarded, did not complete the test. Two others were removed from school following a quarrel between parents and administrators.

Lincoln, Nebraska, at that time. The Native American community in Lincoln is quite close, and all tribal members were personally known to our assistant, Ms. Shirley Cayou, who was active in Native American organizations. We also used raw data from the *Lincoln Indian Census* of 1970 as a guide.[2] Using the census as a source, we visited all the Native American homes which listed children under age six and explained the project to the parents. Ms. Cayou accompanied us, requesting their permission for their children's participation in the research. Through a "snowball" effect, we also found families who had come to Lincoln after the census was taken, and invariably Ms. Cayou knew of moves to town or back to the reservation, as ties between the two communities are close.

On the Nebraska reservation a somewhat different technique was employed. Here, with our reservation assistant, Mr. Oliver Sansoci, we conducted a house-to-house tour of the reservation. As we approached a house, Mr. Sansoci would announce, "Yeh. They got a lotta kids," or, "No kids there." While this may sound like a rather unusual method to those familiar with the New York or Boston telephone directory, it must be understood that in a folk-society like this, each person is known by all others. There was some sample mortality here because of families travelling off the reservation to pow-wows or to visit friends or relatives in town, and also because the protective Mr. Sansoci would not permit us to approach a house where heavy drinking was going on. However, these exceptions were few, and we have obtained nearly a total sample of children between three and five from that Native American community.

The South Dakota sample, although small, represents the population of Head Start students and their preschool siblings from one district of their reservation in southwestern South Dakota. Permission to interview these children was obtained with the help of Vivian One Feather, an educator and community leader. At Ms. One Feather's suggestion, the researcher

2. Margot Liberty, "The Urban Reservation."

demonstrated the test, using her son as "subject," for the consideration of twelve Native American teachers and administrators and explained each question and its implication. This group granted us permission to interview the children. The researcher was advised that other districts on that reservation would not be receptive to the project. A list of the Head Starters was obtained, and two female Native American helpers conducted me to the homes and explained the project to the parents. The children were then interviewed in their homes.

A control group of white children was selected from schools and day care centers in Phoenix, Arizona, and Lincoln, Nebraska. This sample represents children from middle, working, and lower socio-economic groups at day care centers and other schools. A control group was essential if we were to attribute any pattern in the behavior of the Native American children to their Native American status, and not to age, sex, or some other variable. To do this it was necessary to demonstrate how such a pattern compares to that of white children.

Phoenix and Lincoln were selected as locations for obtaining the white sample as they geographically approximate the locations of the southwestern and plains Nebraska tribes, respectively. While no control group of white children was selected from the area immediately adjoining the South Dakota plains reservation, its proximity to Nebraska and the similarity to the general life styles of the people of the two states permitted us to consider the Lincoln white sample as a control for both groups. Both locations are "midwestern" in character. Indeed, some of the parents of the white Lincoln sample were natives of northwest Nebraska, which borders Group 3's reservation.

Doll-Play Technique

Equipment

The dolls used in the interviews were small flexible dolls $3^1/_2$ inches high ("parent dolls" were 5 inches), made in Germany. Each of the twelve pairs of dolls is matched for sex and dress and is identical in all respects except race. As no Native American dolls manufactured could be found which matched the white dolls and still filled the requirements of small size and flexibility, sets of the white dolls were purchased and one-half of them "nativized" by the researcher. Skin was colored a reddish tan of a medium darkness. Hair and eyes were darkened and a slight upward tilt given each eye at the outer corner. Clothing was made for the female dolls, as the manufacturer dresses them all alike, and the demands of our research were that each pair, although dressed like each other, be dressed differently from every other pair. This enables us to ask the subjects to choose from a pair of dolls and isolate race as a variable. Thus the child cannot escape the racial choice by citing dress differences for his or her selection.

We also made different-colored trousers for the little boy dolls. It was not necessary to make clothing for the adult male dolls, as the manufacturer does produce two models of "father," one in plaid suit and tie, and one in shirt sleeves with solid-colored slacks.

The set of dolls tended to become worn with vigorous, although loving, handling. Other doll-playing researchers have found this, too, but our problem was compounded by reservation conditions. Sand and dust which blow continually through the Arizona school buildings—only one of which had any air conditioning in temperatures which reach 118°F.—leave all surfaces covered with a layer of brown film. More traditional Nebraska tribesmen do not ask strangers or casual acquaintances into their homes, so much of the Nebraska interviewing was carried out on the ground outside the home, interviewer and child sitting cross-legged in the dust, amid discarded furniture, car parts and broken toys. This necessitated repeated laundering of doll clothes and application of fresh paint to the Indian dolls. A second set of dolls was purchased for the November interviews, and was, when adapted, identical to the first, which by then had become too worn for further use.

Two dollhouse sets were also prepared specifically for this

research. These are of three-sided, collapsible plywood which can be easily carried and set up. They were built to the scale of the dolls. The first set was a school setting. On one wall was a blackboard, on the other a clock and some stick-figure drawings. This set contained small desklike tables and chairs. The other set was a home scene, with sofa, chair, coffee table, and television set. The furniture was plain and wooden, not unlike the furniture in Native American homes. A window was shown on one wall, and a clock on the other. The entire impression was one of simplicity, so as not to seem too elaborate to poor children.

The Test

The doll-play technique basically involves the child in a story which the interviewer tells.[3] This story sets up situations that deal with choices of people to play roles in the story, and these roles are imbued with social meaning. Like other projective techniques, it allows the subject to treat situations indirectly which he might be reluctant to discuss directly—"What do you think Johnny thinks?" instead of "What do you think?" At several stages in the story, the child is asked to choose from a matched pair of dolls the one he wants to play a certain role in the story. These roles and the choices he makes to fill them tell about his racial stereotyping. Following the structured interview the child is encouraged to play freely with the equipment. The spontaneous arrangements he makes with the dolls and the conversations he creates among them provide us with another source of rich, although less structured, data.

The test has the advantage of being "fun" and not readily perceived as a testing situation; it is, therefore, nonthreatening. It is also not culture-bound. The situations portrayed in the stories are common childhood experiences. As many small children are shy or nonverbal, this test is especially useful in

3. This test is a modified version of that used by Judith D. R. Porter, described in *Black Child, White Child*. A complete text appears in the Appendix.

working with them because children can indicate their choices of dolls by pointing or gesturing. Usually a child soon feels at ease and begins to chatter happily, but in some cases extremely shy children were able to complete the interview quite contentedly without speaking at all. This gives usable data about children who, of necessity, would be excluded from studies that rely on verbal participation such as the TAT and its modifications, or the Rorscach.

The child is asked to come with the interviewer to a quiet place and "play a game." Wherever possible, the interview took place in a quiet room donated by the school for the interview. However, the limited size of reservation buildings and the fact that many schools and homes are one-room, sometimes made it impossible to find a really private place to interview our subjects. The challenges of setting the interview away from other children, all of whom were clamoring for their turns, and of keeping the equipment out of view to preserve its novelty for each successive subject, were met in a variety of ways. Sometimes a quiet corner could be isolated by encircling it with a wall of blocks or chairs. Sometimes the researcher took the child outside the group. When the group was indoors, the interviewer went out, and returned to the classroom when the group went to the play yard. One morning was spent under a table. In the case of home visits, we began to carry some of the old, discarded dolls. Siblings of the subject were taken to a distant area of the yard and encouraged to become involved in play with these old dolls. This usually satisfied the other children's immediate desire to touch the equipment, but did not lessen the novelty of the dollhouse sets and the more brightly dressed and painted dolls used in the test itself. This device also kept the other children out of earshot so that they would not simply imitate the answers of a previously tested brother or sister.

First, the child sat facing the school set. The other set was turned around so that the subject would not be distracted by it or its contents. The dolls were hidden from view between the backs of the two sets. The interviewer asked the child: "Do you like to tell stories? Do you sometimes watch stories on TV?" If the child answered "Yes," the interviewer proceeded: "We're going to pretend we're making up a TV story—like the ones you see on television." Some extremely poor children or some in more isolated areas did not watch television or may have viewed it only occasionally at a relative's home. If this seemed to be the case, the interviewer would simply tell the child that his help was required in "telling a story." Either approach was almost invariably successful in catching the children's interest. It also put them at ease, as all children, especially Native American children, are familiar with stories and storytelling and thus feel themselves on familiar territory. The storytelling then began.

Cards

Drawings in the form of laminated, deck-sized face cards were prepared by an artist for the researcher. Like the dolls, each set of cards was matched for dress and sex; but each set contained three, rather than two, pictures: one Native American, one white, and one black. Four of these sets were heads and shoulders of adults, two of men, and two of women. The rest were children's faces and shoulders. This use of full faces allowed accentuation of racial characteristics such as the fuller mouths of blacks and the almond eyes and high cheekbones of Native Americans. There were two alternatives in the use of the cards. They could be used for the entire test, in place of the dolls, or they could be used in some way in conjunction with the dolls.

These alternatives were tested in the pretest. Ten pairs of southwestern Native American children matched for sex, age, and general economic status were tested. One group was given the test using the choice of three cards at each of the points of choice indicated in the story. The other group was given the doll-play test using dolls. After matching the doll families they were asked to put together card families. Three father cards, one of each race, were placed before the children. Then three mother cards were shown. Indicating the Native American father, the interviewer would ask: "Which woman belongs in his family?" and so on for the other two fathers. In a similar fashion, the child was asked to place a boy and a girl in each of the families. All the cards were picked up, and the interviewer dealt out three correctly matched families, then took up a white doll and asked the child, "Which of the card families does he look like?" Then the child was asked to match a Native American doll of his own sex to a card group.

Several interesting discoveries were made during the pretest. (1) First, the children who had a choice of cards, rather than dolls, in the story did not do significantly better at racial self-selection. In fact, the doll-users chose Native American self-images more often. (2) The presence of three choices seemed to confuse the smaller children, and the cards failed to maintain the intensity of concentration and enthusiasm that are possible with doll play. (3) Most younger children could not successfully create card families. While some could create a complete white family, of husband, wife, son, and daughter, there was considerable mixing up of Indian and black cards. This indicates that most three-year-olds and early fours tend to discriminate on a dark-light basis, without full appraisal of such racial characteristics as lip and eye formation and hair texture.

It was therefore decided to utilize the cards *in addition to* rather than *in place of* the dolls.

We utilized the card-family-making and doll-to-card matching sections of the test after the doll-play interview. These two tests proved to be good indices of racial awareness. The doll-to-card matching test was the most difficult of the operations to perform, and therefore allows us to draw a line between high-awareness children who performed the task and low-awareness youngsters who did not. In addition, it is better as a measure of cognition because it avoids the use of the term "family." As there is much variation in skin color within many Native American families, we cannot put our faith in the doll-family-matching test as a measure of cognition. The child may, in placing a white and dark doll in the same family, be portraying a real situation as he or she has observed it. Such a child would be rated "low-awareness" by the family-matching test— a measure of color matching must be simply that, a measure of the child's ability to put people of the same color together. The use of the term "family" throws a psychological monkey wrench into the child's processing of the interviewer's instructions. However, if he associates the darker doll with the black cards, we are alerted to the fact that he may have perceived the darker doll as Negro and that his pattern of choice may reflect not a rejection of his group but of another out-group.

The child is given several minutes in which to play with the equipment as he wishes, and his actions are noted, as are any spontaneous remarks that might be pertinent to the test. Note was also made of each doll-choice during the test, on a prepared form. Most children were so involved in the story that they did not pay much attention to the note-taking. A few children wanted to know, "What are you writing?" To this the response was given that the interviewer was writing down things to help remember all the details of the "story." This satisfied and, in fact, pleased even the most curious, and the child would return to play and cease, from all appearances, to be concerned with the checking-off process.

What do the various questions indicate to us? We are concerned with three concepts: (1) *Racial self-identification:* the child's choice of Johnny and Bobby, who are described as looking "just like you." (2) *Racial preference:* the child's selection of "friends," "nice children," those who are "pretty and neat," and those who will come home for lunch or receive the last bottle of soda pop, indicating which race the child favors and to which he assigns positive terms; the "lazy and stupid" question taps the opposite sentiment. (3) *Racial awareness:* what cognitive grasp the child has of "race," his ability to place members of a racial group together and recognize their difference from others. Here, as we have indicated, we found the doll-to-picture match to be the most reliable measure. In asking the child to place family members together, and to match doll and card, we measure the child's awareness of race and its meaning.

Interviewers

Because the southwestern North American group is darker than the researcher, over twenty of them were interviewed by a tribal interviewer, as their group might have exhibited interviewer bias. It apparently did not (tables 2 and 3): her results were not significantly different from my own with a similar group of children.

Table 2

Pretest of self-identification of Native American children with tribal and nontribal interviewers

	Tribal Interviewers	Nontribal Interviewer	N
Correct Self-Identification	7	6	12
Incorrect	5	6	12
	12	12	N=24

$\chi^2=.33$ (not significant)

Table 3

Pretest of "Very Nice" stereotype of Native American children with tribal and nontribal interviewers

	Tribal	Nontribal	N
Own Race	4	5	9
Other Race	8	7	15
N=	12	12	N=24

$\chi^2+1.66$ (not significant)

To minimize the effects of "strangeness," I was at all times accompanied by a tribal member familiar to the children and their parents. These guides would explain the study briefly to the parents and put them at ease. They also indicated to the children that the "game" was a pleasant experience.

Reporting the data

The reader will note that as well as describing statistically significant relationships, I have noted certain nonsignificant ones. Because this is the first work of its kind with Native American children, and certain sub-groups are quite small, I hope to point the way to further research by noting tendencies which merit further investigation.

Racial preference was measured by the number of times a child selected a doll of his own racial group for a positive stereotype, or selected a doll of the other race for a negative stereotype. For example, the child was asked to select "the boy people like to play with," the "nice girl," and "the kid they don't like." A child was given a score of $+1$ for a choice of the doll of his own race for a positive stereotype or a doll of the other race for a negative stereotype. For example, suppose in the story we asked the child to pick the doll who is the "lazy and stupid" girl in the story. A Native American child who selected the white doll in this instance would receive a score of $+1$; if he selected the Native American doll, he was scored zero. As there were eight questions which tapped the preference aspect of the children's attitudes, the highest possible score would be $+8$. To facilitate comparison with the Porter data, the "preference scores" were collapsed into three categories—"high" or 3 for children who scored $+7$ or $+8$; "medium" or 2 for those who scored between $+4$ and $+6$; and "low" or 1 for those who scored between 0 and $+3$.

In the case of racial self-identification, the child was told at the beginning of both stories, "This story is about a boy (girl) who looks like you. Which boy (girl) looks like you?" Then the interviewer offered the child two dolls of the child's sex, differing only in skin color. Those children who correctly identified themselves with a doll of their own race both times were given a score of 2. Those who misidentified once or both times received a score of 1. Thus, for a child to be considered a correct identifier, he or she had to show a consistent perception of racial membership and willingness to acknowledge it. One incorrect choice is indicative of ambivalence on the part of the child.

Findings

The most startling results of the projective interviews lie in the areas of racial self-identification and racial preference. Race is an important variable. Native American youngsters are much more likely than whites to select dolls of the opposite race for positive stereotypes, as table 4 indicates. They also identify themselves with the doll of their own race less frequently than do white children (table 5). Thus, it appears from this first series of observations that these children may already have placed a positive value on whiteness within the context

Table 4

Analysis of variance: own-race preference by race

Race	N	Mean Self-Identification Score
White	95	1.90
Native American	117	1.61

N = 212
F = 8.15 (significant at p .01)
lowest score = 1
highest score = 3

Table 5

Analysis of variance: self-identification by race

Race	N	Mean Self-Identification Score
White	95	1.60
Native American	117	1.41

N   =212
F   =8.34 (significant at p. 01)
low =1
high=2

of American society. But to leap to such a conclusion at this point in the analysis would be premature. In the following pages, we shall examine these findings in the light of other results. We shall be concerned specifically with three main issues. (1) To what extent and in what direction does the age of the children influence their responses to racial stereotypy and racial self-identification questions? (2) To what extent does racial awareness influence these responses? (3) To what extent do our more impressionistic data—field notes on classroom behavior, spontaneous remarks made during the session with the interviewer, and the dramas children enacted with the dolls during their free play—confirm or qualify the results of the more structured projective test? In addition, within the Native American group we will examine the influence of parental activism.

The factor which relates most strongly to correct self-identification is race. Table 5 indicates the mean scores of white and Native American children on racial self-identification.

As increasing age exposes children to a wider range of experiences, enlarging their grasp of social roles and expanding their comprehension of racial differences, we should examine the influence of age as a variable on the relationship between race and the dependent variables of self-identification and stereotypy. We might expect older children—regardless of race—to identify themselves more correctly with the doll of their own race than do the three- and four-year-olds. This is true for white children, as is shown by table 6, but it is *not* true for Native American youngsters. Rather, with increasing age is increased the tendency to identify with the white dolls. This would certainly suggest that increased age may have different effects on majority and minority children. The child is learning the difference between racial groups as they exist in a given societal context. The child begins to see that these differences are somehow associated with a hierarchy of social roles in our own society. It becomes more and more apparent that within this hierarchy whites are more likely to assume the privileged and powerful roles, while peoples of color are relegated to low-status and sometimes demeaning positions. Awareness of a social-racial hierarchy leads children of the two groups to respond quite differently to their respective situations and produces the pattern of responses to our self-identification questions which are revealed by the table.

Table 6

Mean racial self-identification scores of Native American and white children of younger and older preschool age groups.

Race	Age	
	3–4	5–low 6
White	1.53	1.84
	(N=76)	(N=19)
Native American	1.43	1.37
	(N=69)	(N=48)
	N =212	
	F Age =2.44 (not significant)	
	F Race =13.55 $p<.001$	
	F Age × Race=5.44 $p<.05$	

For the white child, there is a comforting consistency in the two pieces of new social knowledge. The process looks something like this: I am white → Being white is a good thing in this society → I'm glad I'm white.

For the Native American child the process is different: I am brown → Being white is better in this society than being brown → I would like to be able to live like white people live. There may be some reluctance on the part of the five- or six-year-old Native American to wholeheartedly think of himself or herself as a nonwhite.

It is very important to note here that our "older" children are five and six. There is an indication that this group of children identifies itself less well than did the younger children. However, there is no suggestion here that this is a continuous process which would cause seven-year-olds or nine-year-olds to do even less well. Any conclusions about the older child must await further and thorough research. While there is, in the literature of the Red Power movement and elsewhere, retrospective testimony by adults that as children they had wished to be white, it is unclear at exactly what age these feelings were present and how long they persisted. It is also necessary to once again remind the reader that the tendency of the Native American children in the sample, and of the adults who have confessed to it, to identify themselves with whiteness need not and should not at this time be interpreted as a rejection of own-group membership. It may well be that whiteness is merely an appropriate symbol for a lack of discrimination and a relatively good life. In a later chapter, I suggest a series of stages through which the child passes in acquiring racial attitudes.

That it is the positive imagery associated with white and not necessarily white *qua* white that appeals to the children is attested to by the results of a consideration of the relationship between race, age, and stereotype as shown in table 7. Both groups of children show an increased tendency to associate the white dolls with the positive stereotypes in the story. As the stereotypes used in society were the basis for those used

Table 7

Mean preference scores of Native American and white children
of younger and older preschool age groups

Race	Age	
	3–4	5–low 6
White	1.84 (N=76)	2.15 (N=19)
Native American	1.66 (N=69)	1.54 (N=48)

N	=212
F Age	=1.13 (not significant)
F Race	=19.56 p<.001
F Age × Race	=6.06 p<.01

in the stories, this performance on the part of the children
indicates that they are indeed learning the script of the social
drama in which they will play the "appropriate" roles. They
are learning the social system.

Awareness of Race and Racial Feelings

It could be argued that increasing age represents different
stages in the development of the children of the two races,
that Native American children are too sheltered from the
mainstream of American society to be conscious of racial differences or to understand the social interpretations which are
given these differences in our culture. Therefore, one might
argue, the results of the age-by-race-by-racial-feelings test are
meaningless because increased age need not mean increased
awareness on the part of the children, or if it does mean increased awareness for the two groups, need not mean the same
degree of awareness exists for white children as for Native
Americans. Such an argument could be rephrased, "Older
whites show more positive stereotypy for their own race and
better identification with it than do older Native Americans,

because whites know more about race." Therefore it seems appropriate to consider awareness as a separate variable apart from age in order to determine whether or not this will turn around the results as we have reviewed them to this point. It was decided to use the doll-to-picture match as the primary measure of awareness, as we have noted. This was the most difficult of the tasks for the children to perform and thus represents the most stringent test of their ability to match by race. It also avoids the use of the word "family" which could bias the doll family-matching and the picture family-matching, as children could become confused and interpret those questions as tapping what the people in their own families looked like, rather than a test of ability to match by race.

Tables 8 and 9 examine the responses of high-awareness children only, considered with regard to racial feelings. The more aware white children evince a high degree of own-race identification and positive stereotypy associated with their own group. The reverse is true for the high-awareness Native Americans, who tend to associate positive stereotypy with the other race and to identify with it. Thus, degree of awareness does not alter the overall picture.

Once again we face the indication that the more children

Table 8

One-way analysis of variance:
own-race preference by race for correct doll-to-picture matchers

1=low
2=high

Race	N	Mean Preference Score
White	61	1.85
Native American	48	1.60
	N=109	
	F=4.76	
	P<.04	

Table 9

Racial self-identification by race for correct doll-to-picture matchers

	1=low 2=high	
Race	N	Mean Self-Identification Score
White	61	1.77
Native American	48	1.39
	N=109 F=8.15 P<.01	

know about race in this society, the better white status appears to them.

Self-identification and stereotypy are highly correlated (F = 11.65). Thus, it appears that it is not awareness of racial differences which automatically leads a child to identify with the doll of the correct race, but the images with which that race is associated stereotypically in the child's mind.

Other Evidence

In addition to the structured projective test, recorded observation of the children during a period of free play with the dolls and other equipment was of considerable value to the research. After the storytelling game, each child was told that he or she could use any or all of the testing props and do whatever he or she wanted with them in the testing area. Most children disregarded the cards and focused on the dolls and doll furniture. The remarks the children made about the dolls, and the dramas they enthusiastically and uninhibitedly enacted with them, taught us almost as much about their racial awareness and attitudes as their performances on the test itself. Very important confirmation of the relationship between realization of social roles and the acquisition of racial attitudes can be seen in the acute perception of the role hierarchy of American society which came through in some of the stories.

Many of the children told stories or acted out dramas which placed brown dolls in situations of subservience to white dolls.

Mary, a five-year-old Native American, arranged several of the brown dolls in the living room set—a child sitting on the floor in front of the television, mother and father dolls lying on the sofa. She then selected a white adult female doll and began to make it stomp toward the house. Then she took up the little brown doll from its position before the television set and placed it by the window. "He's lookin' outa the window," Mary tells the interviewer. "He seen that lady comin'. He says, 'Momma! Get up! Here come the social worker!' "

Marty, a six-year-old male Native American from the southwest, shows the interviewer a brown male adult doll. "This guy's drunk. Not hurtin' no one—just lyin' on the sofa. Oh, oh! Here comes the cop. (He holds up white male adult doll.) Gonna' shoot that drunk guy."

Jane, a middle-class white child of five years, is a prim child who appears at school every day in a pastel frock, despite the teacher's urging that pants would be more practical. She is meticulous in her play, placing white dolls on chairs in the living room, taking great pains to make sure that they are all sitting up straight. This requires a great deal of patience, because if they aren't bent in precisely the right places, they have a tendency to fall off their chairs. Once this task is completed, and all the dolls are stiffly seated in a circle, Jane sighs happily and sits back on her heels to survey her accomplishment. The interviewer asks, "Now what? What's going on now?" Jane replies, "They sit there."

> Interviewer (a bit perplexed): "What for? What are they doing?"
>
> Jane: "They're going to talk about life insurance."
>
> Interviewer (indicating pile of unused brown dolls): "What about them?"
>
> Jane: "Uh-uh. They can't come into the living room."

The general atmospheres of the different worlds these children inhabit is also revealed to us in their play. Whites tend to portray rather placid, comfortable (and in some cases boring) activities. The characters in these stories are engaged in children's games, or are playing with favorite toys, which are identified by name ("he's playing with his G.I. Joe"). Some of them are on vacations, or at country clubs or national parks.

Native American children tell stories and enact dramas which reflect the realities of their lives. Their characters drink, they haul water, go to powwows, and visit with relatives. Some of their characters get drunk, fight, and have sex. Illness and fire, never mentioned in white children's stories, were frequent themes in the Native American children's tales. The child, Jane, discussed above, probably *does* live in a comfortable but slightly dull world of formally seated people and life-insurance policies. On the southwestern reservation, on the other hand, where only government and missionary buildings had water, children told stories of hauling water, or of fires that destroyed houses.

Certainly it is not only such physical realities which the children reveal to us through their drama. The social hierarchies, which are both cause and consequences of the physical circumstances of their lives, do not escape the attention and comprehension of the Native American youngsters.

Marty created a dramatic scenario replete with fights, drinking, and a little sex, to boot. The crescendo of the drama was a fire which sent the occupants of the living room fleeing out-of-doors. Although dolls of both colors had been in the living room, Marty now made a grouping of only the brown dolls and simulated the sound of sobbing.

> Interviewer: "I guess they're really sad about the house, huh?"
> Marty: "Yeah. They cryin'."
> Interviewer (points to the white dolls that had been in the living room): "What about them?"
> Marty: "They not cryin'. They got another house. Even got water."

Many Native American children created school scenes in their free play with the dolls. All of them used a predominance of brown dolls for the pupils, but without exception they all used white dolls for the teacher. This is not too surprising if we consider that all of them had white teachers, but it was a bit perplexing because many of the classrooms had several Native American women who were assistants to the teachers. I had thought, and I am sure many of the policy makers had thought, that this was a way of providing adult Native Americans in desirable roles for the children to emulate. Why, then, had the children not placed some brown teacher dolls in their dramas? The answer came to me through the help of a five-year-old boy, Dom, with whom I had this conversation.

    Dom (holding up white doll): "The children's all here and now the teacher's coming in."

    Interviewer: "Is that the teacher?"

    Dom: "Yeah."

    Interviewer (holding up a brown doll): "Can she be the teacher?"

    Dom: "No *way!* Her's just a *aide.*"

The presence of Native American women had not for a minute prevented this child from a full comprehension of the real power relations that existed in his school. He *knew* who was running the show.

These examples reveal to us the amazingly accurate grasp that children have of the prevailing social hierarchies in our society. This evidence will, ironically, be doubted by many who take for granted the once highly inflammatory concept of infantile sexuality. Now, we are willing to acknowledge that small children are sexual beings but not that they are political beings. Just as sexuality was the predominant taboo of Freud's time, the acknowledgment of the unequal distribution of power may be that of ours.

Within the Native American Group

Neither social class, area of the country, tribe, or the appearance of the child had a consistent influence on the children's choices for positive roles or on their selection of self-images. However, within the Native American group, there did appear two nonsignificant but highly consistent trends which raise important questions and should provide the material for further research in these areas.

Parental Activism

We considered an "active" parent one who held tribal office, took a leadership role in such social and ceremonial events as dances at the urban Indian center, powwows or giveaways, was a religious leader or active layperson in traditional tribal religion or the Native American Church, or actively participated in organizations whose declared *raison d'être* is the betterment of conditions for Native Americans. Belonging to an organization alone was not qualification for being categorized as active: the person had to be involved to the extent of attending meetings, taking part in group projects, and spending time and energy on the cause.

Few of the parents were engaged in such activity, which handicaps our ability to accurately interpret the data. However, we can say that, in general, the children of two activist parents performed better on the racial self-identification and the stereotypy indices than other Native American youngsters (tables 9, 10, 11).

Table 10

Analysis of variance: Native American children's own-race preference by parental activism

1=low
3=high

Parental Activism	N	Mean Score
None	91	1.63
One Parent	19	1.42
Both Parents	7	1.85

N=117
F=2.05 (not significant)

Table 11

Analysis of variance: Native American self-identification
by parental activism

1=low
2=high

Parental Activism	N	Mean Self-Identification Score
None	91	1.36
One Parent	19	1.39
Both Parents	7	1.71

N=117
F=1.44 (not significant)

Such children are being socialized in an environment which has several aspects conducive to the formation of a positive image of the Native American group. First, these are two-parent families where harmony and activity are the norms. Because of their involvement in a common cause, the parents have little time to spend quarreling with one another or with their children. Thus, they may be more likely to produce a happy home environment in which their children can grow.

Second, these families stress in the socialization of their children the positive aspects of membership in the Native American group. Ceremonies and festivals with their attendant anticipation and excitement come to figure prominently in the lives of children in such homes. Therefore, being Native American has many positive associations for them. A black psychiatrist, Alvin Poussaint, has stressed the importance of parental approval of own-group membership. In a recent article in Ebony, he took the position that, while whites certainly do not provide the only models for black youngsters, parents cannot sit back and let nature take its course. Rather, they must play an active role, conscientiously conveying positive images of their racial group to their children.[4] Child psychiatrist Phyllis Harrison-Ross also urges deliberate inculcation of values which stress the positive qualities of the child's own racial group.[5] White values are too pervasive, these clinicians warn, to be left unchallenged by the parents.[6] Our data are admittedly scant, primarily because of the small number of activist parents, but do suggest that a parental attitude (especially when shared by both parents) of positive identification with the racial group and a participation in group activities transmit a more favorable image of the group to the child.

The Urban Native American Child

While researchers of adult Native Americans living in urban centers have indicated that they are undergoing a renewal of identification with their group and Pan-Indianness, our data indicate that city life is more difficult for the children involved. Holding tribe constant and comparing the Nebraska Native American reservation and urban children, a tendency appears for the urban youngsters to identify with the brown dolls less often than the reservation youngsters and to show more positive stereotypy for the white dolls (tables 12 and 13). Children in the urban environment are cut off from many ethnic events; they may be teased at school, ostracized in the neighborhood. In addition, they are more likely to be exposed to the negative manner in which the culture portrays Native Americans, especially television cartoon characters.

That this trend exists suggests that the urban situation which adds prejudicial discrimination to institutional racism is more conducive to the formation of negative attitudes towards one's own group, or at least, an inflated assessment of

4. Alvin Pouissant, "Building a strong self-image in the Black child." *Ebony* (August 1974): 136-43.

5. Phyllis Harrison-Ross, *The Black Child: A Parent's Guide* (New York: Peter H. Wyden, 1973).

6. The role such teaching plays in shattering the consistency of cultural ideologies is discussed in the conclusion.

Table 12

Own-race preference by residence

1=low
3=high

Residence	N	Mean Preference Score
Urban	21	1.57
Reservation	21	1.68
	N=42 F=.45 (not significant)	

Table 13

Self-identification by residence

1=low
2=high

Residence	N	Mean Self-Identification Score
Urban	21	1.33
Reservation	21	1.50
	N=42 F=1.20 (not significant)	

whiteness, than the reservation situation where institutional racism is less likely to be accompanied by unpleasant face-to-face incidents.

Yet, that the trend is not a significant one suggests the strong influence of institutional racism alone. The reservation child, insulated from the psychologically harmful blows which are inflicted in discriminatory situations, has still learned the significance of being a Native American in white society.

Summary of Preschool Data

In this section we have examined the results of our interviews with Native American and white preschool children. The findings indicate that Native American children tend to associate positive imagery with the other race. Racial self-identification is influenced in a similar manner.

A consideration of the children's use of the dolls during the free-play time supports the contention that children of both races, by the age of four or five, have come to perceive that Native Americans and whites are not only different but that there is a power-prestige component to the relation between the races in our society.

Taken as a whole this body of data suggests that the Native American child is an accurate observer of the social world and comes to realize quite early in life the devalued status of his ethnic group.

Within the Native American group, the children of activists and reservation children show a slightly more positive attitude toward their own racial group than do the children of non-activists and urban-dwelling Native Americans.

A Serendipitous Experiment

Although older children were not included in the projective testing, there are two sources upon which we can base some tentative conclusions about their attitude concerning race and its social meaning. This is useful, because the work which has been done with other minority groups indicates that while young children do indeed evince a preference for white and a tendency to identify with it, older children (seven years and older) seem to have positive feelings about their own racial group. The one study which has been done on Native American children's racial attitudes suggests that this may be the case with this group as well. Thus, although the older children were not of key interest to us, there are several points I should like to make regarding my observations of their feelings about racial matters.

The first source upon which I can draw are my informal observations of the older children in the societies included in the study. In almost every home I visited, there were older siblings, cousins, and their friends who related to me with ease and talked about racial matters. These older children expressed great pride in their Native American identity. They were not unaware of the disfavor in which their group was held. However, they simply did not accept the image of their group that was propagated by the majority culture. A feeling of group solidarity and pride was somewhat stronger in both of the plains tribes than in the southwestern group. In view of subsequent militancy and rebellion which began to emerge in the plains area only months after the first part of the research was completed, and which has continued to the present time, it may safely be assumed that resentment against whites and their treatment of Native Americans was already deeply felt and was taking the form of pride in the in-group, as well as rejection of the standards and prejudices of the majority group. The linguistic format of many remarks in this regard took the form of "whites say . . . but I say. . . ." This pattern was repeated in all three cultures and represents, I believe, the core characteristic of the older children's outlook, which is a realization of their lower status in white eyes and a rejection of the white appraisal. Thus a young girl will say, "Whites think Indians are wild and crazy, but I tell them that's a bunch of crap." "Whites think we're dirty, but I know I'm clean."

This form of reassurance also is used to salve the wounded feelings of younger siblings. One teenager told me that her sister had come home in tears because the white teacher had brought a Native American record to school and the other children had danced around this Native American child warwhooping. "I told her, look, they want to make you feel like you're no good, but they are the ones who's no good. White people got no manners."

Dating a white was not regarded as a status symbol, but was cause for a good deal of negative sanctioning from the peer group. However, this is not a blanket prejudice, and most children distinguished between whites who were "good guys" and those who were not.

The teenagers were keenly aware of the prejudice against them, a fact which made them invaluable aides to the sociologist. It was they who told me that I would be closely watched in stores if I wore any jewelry or clothing which might lead shopkeepers to identify me as a Native American. This wisdom was imparted to me after I told a group of people that a person had followed me up and down the aisles of a store in a Nebraska border town. I had been trying to comprehend his behavior, which I had resented solely as a violation of personal space. The group who heard of this incident listened politely, and then one young woman asked, "Did you have on those moccasins and braid holders?" When I nodded, the entire group burst into laughter. "What did you expect, lady? They think all us Indians shoplift. They follow us around all the time. You better wear something else when you go shopping next time."

The fact that these children knew that they were living in a racist situation and had the good sense and emotional stability not to blame themselves for it does not mean that the situation did not cause them pain. It often did. They would tell one another of incidents that had occurred and express their feelings of anger, sadness, and embarrassment. Hearing a teacher speak with contempt of the Native American group, having the chair next to oneself left vacant at a laundromat or crowded movie, being pointed at by giggling whites, were events these children held deep in themselves and could recount in minute detail even when the event was many months, or even years, in the past.

The possibility of some change occurring was a cherished dream. In some it took the form of a common sense determination to do well in school, go to college and qualify for a job that could be profitable but also could be performed on the reservation. These children wished to improve their life-styles without having to live in the white world. In others, an almost chiliastic belief in the imminent restoration of the land to the Native Americans clung on as it had in their grandparents. A popular song of the time discussed the plight of Native Americans and concluded with the belief in the return of indigenous people to the power and autonomy they once knew. I knew that this was a favorite song with many of the children, as they often spoke of it, but I initially underestimated the depth of feelings which it tapped. One morning, however, I was visiting a home and talking to a group of older children while I waited for my preschool subject to eat her cereal. Suddenly about three people "ssh'd" the rest of us with some vehemence. *The record* was playing on the local radio station. We all sat in absolute silence as the record played. The children tapped their feet or nodded in rhythm with the music but their faces were solemn, their eyes on the floor. When the song ended and the disc jockey prattled again, one girl whispered to me, "We never talk when that song is on."

Still others have begun to affiliate with groups espousing political action on behalf of their people. Many of those who marched on the BIA in Washington and who occupied the village of Wounded Knee, South Dakota, were in their teens.

Thus, informal observations reveal little or no desire to identify as white on the part of older children. While there is an awareness that whiteness and some positive qualities such as wealth, power, and material belongings are often correlated, Native American children of this age do not see these as inherent in whiteness itself, but perceptively recognize these correlations as the product of a social system which has favored whites while discriminating against other groups.

The second set of observations of older children comes from the "serendipitous" experiment mentioned in the subtitle of this section. When can an experiment be serendipitous? When the behavior that emerges as a piece of data was originally engaged in for other purposes, unrelated to the problem under investigation.

One of the problems I frequently encountered in the interviewing was that of older children who were not to be included in the study. Since the test was fun and the younger children were obviously having a very good time, older children, having been cautioned not to come too close and distract the smaller subject, would stand at the edges of the testing area and watch intently, trying to see what we were about, to catch a question, or to glimpse what we did with the equipment. If they saw me arrive at a school or neighborhood days after they had first seen me, they would ask to be tested. I explained that the study really concerned the attitudes of little children, and said I would play other games with the older children when I finished the testing, but they seemed unsatisfied, and I felt guilty. It seemed to me, as I thought it out one evening, that it was an abuse of Native American hospitality to leave any member of the group unhappier for my presence on the reservation or in the urban neighborhood. Therefore, I decided to find a way of making the older children feel more a part of the work I was doing.

The reason that older children had been excluded from the testing situation as observers was that they might bias the responses of the actual subjects through expressions of disapproval and attempts to coach the smaller children. Also, I feared that if they observed the test, they would tell younger children who had not yet been tested about it and give them instructions on the responses. However, it occurred to me that after the younger children in a community had been tested, I could allow the older children to observe me testing one of the younger three-year-old children, whose case would then be excluded from the data. Under these conditions, no restrictions would be placed on the verbal expressions of the older children, and they could play with the equipment after the interview was completed. Thus, I began to hold these "group interviews" with older children to prevent them from feeling excluded from my work.

What happened was that I learned a great deal from their remarks and behavior at these sessions. In their urgings for the young "subject" to choose a brown doll for every positive stereotype and a white doll for the "lazy and stupid kid" in the story, their own feelings concerning Native American identity emerged in an impressive fashion. There were two types of behavior which were of particular interest and which differed from group to group. However, every group took one of these two approaches to their roles as participant-observers.

The first type of response was the "active" mode of response. The older children in an active group would furiously urge the smaller child on to what they considered correct doll-selection, and also gave instructions on the awareness items, attempting to make the subject score perfectly on the color-matching items. Quite aware that the "proper" selection for a "pretty and nice" stereotype was a brown doll, and that the brown doll matched the Native American and not the black picture, these children were openly appalled by an "incorrect" choice on the part of the subject. "No, no, Sister! Not that one! No! Take the brown one! Take the Indian!" Some of these "active" group members went so far as to snatch a doll deemed "incorrect" from the younger child's hand and to re-place it with the doll of the opposite color. These children saw their role vis-à-vis the younger children in the community as one of instructor and active intervener. The solidarity of their own peer group had provided a bulwark against the injuries of racism, and they soon would allow the younger child to become a part of that group. This instructional capacity of the older children with regard to racial attitudes is probably a very real factor in everyday life that is not readily observable by social scientists. However, the game of "doing the doll choice" brought this capacity to the fore. I believe that the role of peer instruction has been underestimated in attempts to understand the development of racial attitudes and the changes in those attitudes that can occur with increasing age. In the following chapter, I suggest some of the functions of this learning from peers in the establishment of correct racial identity.

The second type of behavior was "subtle-intimidative."

These children watched the test as if it were an important football game. The atmosphere was full of silent excitement as the group waited in suspense for the subject's choice. The participants kept mental scores. A child whispers to herself, "He picked three white ones." The children's bodies become tense as another question is posed. "Which is the boy that John wants to take home for lunch?" All eyes are on the subject, who considers the matter with great deliberation, eyeing the white and Native American dolls in my hand. Her hand begins to go toward the white doll. There is the sound of many children taking in a sharp breath of air in unison. Frowning, she looks around her at the faces of brother, sisters, and many friends. She grins, laughs, and her hand grasps the brown doll. There is a great exhalation of breath, and the little forms simultaneously relax. Their communication to her has been nonverbal, subtle, but it conveys the same message to her that a more active and vociferous group would have conveyed.

In all cases, the younger children were urged in some way to show a good opinion of their group, as well as to score high on color matching and thus show the researcher that they were "smart."

The strong own-race preference and self-identification in the older children (those nine and over) contrasts with the preference for white and identification with it which we find in the younger children, and demands explanation, as does their ability to hold on to positive own-group attitudes in face of increased understanding of the unequal arrangements which characterize American social life.

The following chapter will attempt to explain these trends and to couch them in terms of a broader theory of racial-attitude development which can increase our understanding of children's racial preference and identification in general.

CHAPTER 4

Towards a Theory
of the Development
# of Racial Attitudes

———◆◆◆———

Children's Racial Attitudes: Past Research

For nearly forty years, researchers have attempted to understand the processes by which children "learn prejudice."
These researchers have concerned themselves with the extent
to which children are aware of racial attitudes and what feelings they have about their own and other races.

Awareness

At first it was believed that children did not form racial attitudes or become concerned with racial differences until well
into the elementary-school years. Bruno Lasker, writing in
1929, maintained that children did not hold racial attitudes

until the age of eight.[1] His study was based on retrospective testimony of adult subjects, which probably accounts for this very high age-estimate. However, Gessell and Ilg also set the age of racial concern quite high, placing it at about ten.[2]

A parent of inquiring children could have informed social scientists that children become interested in racial matters a good deal earlier than eight or ten. It may well be that, while all children in an earlier time became curious about race at around eight, the age of awareness may have gone down because of the advances in the communications industry in the past two decades. In earlier times, there were probably many young children who had no exposure to people of races other than their own. Now, however, television presents them with people of various races at an early age. Later researchers began to find evidence which contradicted the earlier theories about the development of race awareness. In the late 1930s, Ruth Horowitz indicated that nursery-school children did have an awareness of racial differences, and the Clarks' studies demonstrated racial awareness in black children as young as three years. Mary Ellen Goodman's work with four-year-olds indicated a spectrum of awareness in children of the same chronological age: some children are highly aware of race, while others seem moderately aware and still others only vaguely aware of such differences. Morland's work with black and white children supported the other studies.[3]

1. Bruno Lasker, *Race Attitudes in Children* (New York: Holt and Company, 1929), p. 67.

2. Arnold Lucius Gessell and Frances Lillian Ilg, *The Child From Five to Ten* (New York and London: Harper and Brothers, 1946), pp. 338, 356-58.

3. Ruth Horowitz, "Racial Aspects of Self-Identification in Nursery School Age Children," *Journal of Psychology* 7 (1939): 91-99; Kenneth Clark and Mamie Clark, "The Development of Consciousness of Self and the Emergence of Racial Identification in Negro Pre-School Children," *Journal of Social Psychology* 10 (1939): 591-99; and "Racial Identification and Preference in Negro Children," *Readings in Social Psychology,* ed. Maccoby, Newcomb, and Hartley (New York: Henry Holt and Company, 1958), pp. 602-11; Mary Ellen Goodman, *Race Aware-*

Preference

Most of these researchers also have been concerned with the attitudes associated with racial differences once they are realized. Of especial interest have been the "preference" or stereotype component and the factor of racial self-identification.

In determining preference, most researchers have presented children with a set of positive or negative traits and then asked them to choose either a black or a white person (as represented by dolls or pictures) as filling that description. For instance, a researcher may show a child pictures of a black and a white child and ask, "Which one of these girls is nice and really fun to play with?"

The results of this research, including the Clarks' work, Morland's studies, and the research of Asher and Allen, Goodman, and Horowitz indicate that children of both races show a tendency to associate positive imagery with white. Springer's work with Oriental children in Hawaii showed similar results. A more recent study in Boston, carried out by Porter, has yielded such findings also, but has in addition pointed to the sociological variables which affect children's preferences. Porter found that the social class, sex, and skin color of black children all have an influence on children's choices for positive stereotypes.[4]

---

ness in *Young Children* (Cambridge, Mass.: Addison-Wesley Press, 1952; 2d ed. New York: Collier Books, 1964), pp. 50-73; Kenneth Morland, "Racial Recognition by Nursery School Children in Lynchburg, Virginia," *Social Forces* 37 (1958): 132-37, and "Comparison of Racial Awareness in Northern and Southern Children," *American Journal of Orthopsychiatry* 26 (1966): 22-32.

4. Clark and Clark, "Development of Consciousness" and "Racial Identification"; Morland, "Racial Recognition" and "Comparison of Racial Awareness"; Steven Asher and Vernon Allen, "Racial Preference and Social Comparison Processes," *Journal of Social Issues* 25 (1969): 157-66; Goodman, *Race Awareness*; Horowitz, "Racial Aspects"; Doris Springer, "Awareness of Racial Differences by Pre-School Children in Hawaii," *Genetic Psychology Monographs* 41 (1950): 323-34; and Porter, *Black Child, White Child*, pp. 30-39.

Racial Self-Identification

Porter notes that "the process of self-identification involves at least two components: the perception by a child that he belongs to a group and his willingness to admit this fact."[5] Whether perception or acceptance of membership in a racial group is the primary component of racial self-identification, many studies of preschool children have indicated that white is the preferred racial status in tests of self-identification. The Clarks found that even though nine out of ten black children were aware of racial differences, only six out of ten correctly identified themselves as "Negro."[6] Morland and Goodman also found that many black subjects tended to identify themselves as white.[7] Porter found that, while there was little difference between children of the two races on awareness measures, both groups tended to select white dolls for positive stereotypes and for self-identification.[8]

In racial self-identification as in preference, there are variables, other than race, that can make a difference in a child's response. The Clarks cite age as a variable in this regard, stating that by age seven most black children choose to identify themselves as black, while smaller children may identify themselves as white.[9] Porter found that social class was an important variable in influencing self-identification; middle-class blacks, standing in a marginal position between black and white society, may seek to attain whiteness and thus identify themselves as white.[10]

Similar results have been obtained by Gregor and McPherson working in the Union of South Africa. These researchers showed white and urban and rural Bantu children brown and white dolls on a table, and asked such questions as "which one would you like to play with?" and "which one looks most

---

5. Ibid., p. 86.
6. Clark and Clark, "Racial Identification."
7. Morland, "Racial Recognition"; and *Race Awareness*.
8. Porter, *Black Child, White Child*, pp. 36-39.
9. Clark and Clark, "Racial Identification."
10. Porter, *Black Child, White Child*, pp. 85-86.

like you?" It was found that rural Bantu children identified themselves better than urban Bantu, but that they also showed a stronger preference for white dolls than did their urban counterparts. In all events, white children evinced greater own-race identification and more preference for their own race than did the Bantu children.[11]

Only one study has directed its attention to Native American children's perceptions of race. Bernard Rosenthal, using line drawings of white and light- and dark-brown children, studied racial preference and self-identification among Chippewa children in 1974.[12] His findings indicate that Native American youngsters may suffer from the pervasive racial imagery of white superiority as black children do. Rosenthal reports that children of all ages show preference for the white figures. While small children do not do this so frequently, from the age of five on there is a definite tendency in this direction. Five is a time at which a jump in this tendency occurs—a finding compatible with the work on other minority groups, which has found five to be a peak age for white preference. Rosenthal also found that older children, while still in the majority showing preference for white, do so with less frequency around the ages of nine to ten.[13] This is similar to the drop-off in white preference which has been observed in black youngsters, although the switch to own-race preference occurs a bit earlier in the black children.[14] Rosenthal found good racial awareness in his subjects, which indicates that the preference for white and the tendency he found for children to identify with white cannot be attributed to a lack of racial awareness on the part of Native American youngsters.[15] Rosenthal's work represents

11. A. James Gregor and D. Angus McPherson, "Racial Preference and Ego Identity Among White and Bantu Children in the Republic of South Africa," *Genetic Psychology Monographs* 73-74 (1966): 218-53.

12. Bernard Rosenthal, "Development of Self-Identification in Relationship to Attitudes Towards the Self in the Chippewa Indians," *Genetic Psychology Monographs* 90 (1974): 44-141.

13. Ibid., p. 117.

14. See, for example, Clark and Clark, "Racial Identification."

15. Rosenthal, "Self-Identification in Chippewa Indians," p. 118.

the first attempt to describe Native American children's responses to the environment in terms of race, and it is also ground-breaking in its emphasis on the life conditions of the Chippewa as causal agents in the low racial self-esteem he found. However, it would have been of great use to social scientists interested in this field if he had treated more than one variable at a time. Such questions as what relationship exists between preference and self-identification are difficult to answer when each of the factors is treated separately.

The importance of the Rosenthal study lies in its suggestion that internalization of the cultural message of white superiority is not limited to the black minority, and that, indeed, the face-to-face hurts which we have called prejudicial discrimination are not necessary for a poor racial self-image. If reservation children, sheltered from such slurs, can still be found to show marked preference for white and a tendency to identify with it, combined with high racial awareness, then we must look to the social structure itself—to institutional racism and its meaning for the minority-group child—to fully understand the influence on children's feelings of being nonwhite in a white society.

These studies have been interpreted by some social scientists as indications that the minority-group child suffers adverse psychological effects from his or her position as a stigmatized person in a predominantly white social system. Such psychological effects are often viewed as pervasive and widespread, having an impact on almost every aspect of the psychic and social lives of children. Self-esteem, especially, is believed to be dealt a harsh blow by the existing societal attitudes. Porter has called this set of interpretations the "mark of oppression" theory of racial self-identification.[16] This name is derived from the Kardiner and Ovesey book of the same name, which painted a dismal picture of minority-group personality as almost a total *reaction* to white oppression.[17]

16. Porter, *Black Child, White Child*, p. 175.
17. Abram Kardiner and Lionel Ovesey, *The Mark of Oppression* (New York: Meridian Books, 1952).

The mark of oppression school interprets the preference that minority-group children have shown for white, in tests such as the one used in this study, as a rejection of their true racial identity, an escape into fantasy to avoid association with an oppressed group. Realizing that his or her group is deemed somehow inferior to the dominant group, the child comes to accept and internalize the beliefs and values of that dominant group himself or herself. This dislike for the minority group may be translated into self-hatred. The child then uses a fantasy identification to escape self-hatred, as well as the unpleasant connotations that correct racial self-identification may bring with it. Those who adhere to this explanation tend to believe that the child suffers deep psychological trauma—the result of racial tensions or verbal slurs—and that these inflict long-lasting scars on the personalities of minority-group members. In sum, this school holds to the view that the minority-group member in this society is likely to be sick.

The "color blind" school of thought, on the other hand, rejects race as an important variable in the formation of personality. These thinkers believe that the minority-group member is no more (and no less) likely to suffer psychological trauma than a white person. Mental health or the lack of it is believed to be rooted in childhood events, mother-child interaction, toilet-training, and Oedipal conflicts and the manner in which they are resolved, not in the individual's position in society. Thus, some researchers who have worked with minority-group children even in stressful situations claim to have found no evidence of personality damage in their subjects.

Coles and Ellison reject the idea that black personality is exclusively a reaction to whites and their values.[18] These writers stress positive feelings concerning the self and feelings of personal efficacy on the part of minority-group members.

18. Robert Coles, *Children of Crisis* (Boston: Little Brown, 1967), pp. 316, 326, 330; also Ralph Ellison, *Shadow and Act* (New York: New American Library, 1966), p. 119.

Porter suggests that there may be substance to both theories and that their error lies in a faulty belief that they are describing the same phenomenon, while they are in fact addressing themselves to two separate dimensions of feelings about the self.[19] Pointing out that racial self-identification and personal self-esteem are different, although interrelated, components of personality, Porter suggests that the first group of theorists, the mark of oppressionists, have tapped feelings about racial membership, while the color-blind school, composed mainly of writers concerned with the individual, have examined primarily the individual's sense of self-worth as a person.[20] This latter component may be affected by prejudice, but is primarily acquired through interaction with the immediate environment during childhood, the degree of emotional support offered by significant others, and the ability to effectively cope with novel situations. Thus, it is quite possible for the minority-group child of caring and sensible parents to acquire a good sense of self-esteem and personal efficacy, no matter how he may come to think of the status of his race vis-à-vis whites.

However, as life progresses, these factors cannot remain totally separate, and this is where the color-blind school must be criticized. Discrimination and lack of access to desirable roles in the society are bound to have some effect on personality. To say that people have successfully adjusted to such circumstances is not a radical stance, although some would have us believe it is. Recently we have become aware that adjustment and health are not necessarily the same thing.[21] To say that minority-group people have happily adjusted to their situation and are impervious to all that goes on in the white society is (1) not empirically verified in the face of the pervasiveness of white-controlled communication networks,

19. Porter, *Black Child, White Child*, p. 181.
20. Ibid., p. 192.
21. Adjustment has been criticized as the road to ultimate tyranny by Herbert Marcuse in *One Dimensional Man* and recently by feminist authors such as Shulamith Firestone (*The Dialectic of Sex*) and Phyllis Chesler (*Women and Madness*).

and (2) an insult to minority people because it implies that the only way they can obtain sanity and secure identification is by becoming completely insensible to the situational and historical conditions in which they live. This is particularly ironic, because the criticism color-blind theorists direct against the idea that minority groups are affected by the dominant culture is that minorities are seen only as reactors, and negative reactors at that. Yet they themselves posit that to know about the white world or to be influenced by it is a "bad thing" for the minority-group member. In short, they assume that the minority-group member will, if he or she is influenced at all, be poorly influenced, feel inferior. Yet this need not be the case. It would seem that it is quite possible for a minority-group member to examine white values and ways and find them lacking in comparison to those of his own group. Surely this has been the case in the past. Historians report, for instance, that Plains Indian women, far from being impressed by or envious of white pioneer women, were repulsed by their ways, especially their child-rearing practices, amazed at the severe discipline of a people who "make their own children cry." There are many ways in which blacks, also, can regard whites with something short of mad jealousy. Alvin Poussaint indicates:

> Contrary to popular opinion, white society is not the black youth's only "looking glass." Most black youths grow up in a black community which does not totally accept the definition given it by the white community. . . . Blacks have not really believed that white equals goodness and purity. Their self-concept has never entirely been controlled by whites. They frequently have seen whites as hypocrites who could not be trusted. Blacks have struggled hard to show their children that the white view of blacks as inferior is incorrect as well as immoral.[22]

Nonetheless, Poussaint feels that parents must act to offset the effects of the white culture's definition of blacks. A good

22. Alvin F. Poussaint, "Building a Strong Self-Image," p. 139.

self-concept will not emerge "naturally," but requires concerted effort on the part of the child's socializers.

I will suggest that the preference for white and the desire to identify with it can better be explained as the product of institutional arrangements than as rejection of one's own racial membership. It may very well be that minority-group children do not view white as intrinsically better than brown, black, or red, but rather that they understand that certain societal avenues are better open to those who *are* white. Choosing white, then, may not be choosing white *qua* white, but white as representative of life without poverty, of good health, and of self-determination. This interpretation avoids the "minority as mentally ill" bias of the mark of oppressionists, as well as the "ignorance is bliss" bias of the color-blind school.

Another factor which may account for different impressions of the effect of minority-group status on personality is the different ages of children with whom researchers have worked. Those who have worked with preschoolers have consistently found a high value placed on whiteness in their minority-group subjects, while this phenomenon is much less pronounced in children of elementary-school age. The Clarks, who have worked with children of both age groups, found a difference which confirms this tendency. Their interpretation of these findings was that the preschool child, realizing the preferred status of whites in our society, attempts to extricate himself or herself from a despairing situation by fantasizing himself or herself white.[23] The older child has come to accept the reality of his or her racial situation and freely acknowledges his or her racial status. This "well, I'm black and I'm stuck with it" interpretation of the data may have some substance, but is extremely difficult to verify empirically. Another possible interpretation of the same data is that the maturing child becomes cognitively more sophisticated in his or her concepts of society. While the younger child's concept of race may be bound up with ideas about poverty, living conditions, and political power, the older child differentiates between the

23. Clark and Clark, "Racial Identification."

two sets of variables and realizes that blackness is not intrinsically part and parcel of a deprived life-style. He realizes that
there are poor whites and middle-class blacks. Therefore he
need not deny his membership in the racial group simply
because he wishes to identify with a decent life-style. The role
of peers in generating a positive sense of racial self-identification during elementary school should also not be overlooked
as a factor in this regard.

In summary, studies of racial attitudes in other minority-
group children have revealed a tendency for preschool children to select white as the positive stereotype and the preferred social status. Interpretations of this have been varied,
with some social scientists viewing such data as proof of
deep-lying psychological scarring and others denying that it
really exists at all, with many more moderate interpretations
falling on the spectrum in between. Considering the consistency in these findings and their replication in a number of
studies, there seems little reason to doubt the data themselves.
We must instead pay more attention to the manner in which
we explain what they mean. I have suggested that while it is
foolish to assert that life in a white-dominated society has no
effect on the minority-group child, there are alternatives to
seeing the effects as deeply psychological in nature. Rather,
we can interpret the data on white preference and identification as an understanding on the part of the child of the
existing relations between the races in society. Since most
children, like most other people, want a good life, some power,
and freedom of choice, they may evince a preference for
white because it is associated with those benefits in their
minds. Such behavior should probably not be interpreted as
rejection of own-race membership or as low personal self-
esteem.

Components of the Theory

There are four additional concepts which, together with
our data, indicate that neither the mark of oppression nor the

color-blind theory is adequate for explaining the attitudes of minority group children, although both contain elements which can prove helpful in the search for an explanation. These four concepts can, I believe, shed further light on the children's choices and, hopefully, add to our understanding of the formation of minority-group children's attitudes about their racial status. First, I shall describe these concepts and then indicate how they can help us interpret both the data presented here and the results of studies of minority-group youngsters in general.

Institutional-Cultural Racism

Institutional racism, the reader will recall, was defined in an earlier chapter as "the byproduct of certain institutional practices which operate to restrict on a racial basis the choices, rights, mobility and access of groups of individuals."[24] This restriction functions to keep minority-group persons in over-all life conditions inferior to whites. It is augmented by discriminatory treatment of the group by the culture. Our discussion of the world in which the Native American child lives certainly indicates that that world is one characterized by institutionalized racism. To compound these structural factors, the culture—books, comics, texts, television, movies—all convey the image of the Native American as a past-tense savage or an "intuitive," naive child of nature. The Native American youngster as well as the majority child is exposed to this culture.

Nonconscious Ideology

The concept of institutional racism is closely related to the concept of a nonconscious ideology, a term coined by psychologist Daryl Bem. In the formation of a nonconscious ideology, all of an individual's reference groups concerning a social object (or a group of people) "give off" the same set of messages concerning the nature of that object (or group of people). No contradictory message intrudes upon this unfortunate consistency to make the individual question the accuracy of the image he or she has received. The following quotation from Bem's work makes clear the connection between institutional racism and the formation of a nonconscious ideology.

> But what happens if all his [an individual's] reference groups agree, when his religion, his family, his peers, his teachers and the mass media all disseminate the same message? The consequence is a non-conscious ideology, a set of beliefs and attitudes which he accepts implicitly, but which remains outside his awareness because alternative conceptions of the world remain unimaginable.[25]

Nonconscious ideologies and their formation are tied to institutional racism because it is through the consistency of the racial hierarchy so visible in white institutions and the consistency of the presentation of minority groups in the cultural transmitters that a society is able to disseminate a distorted picture of what the world and its various inhabitants are "really like." To the extent that minority groups remain unrepresented in major roles in our institutions and are misrepresented by the culture, the ability of those in our society to envision an alternative arrangement to our present system of racial inequality is impaired. The connection between institutional racism and nonconscious ideology becomes clearer if, keeping the definition of institutional racism in mind, we ponder what Bem goes on to say:

> A society's ability to inculcate this kind of ideology into its citizens is the most subtle and most profound form of social influence to challenge because it remains invisible.[26]

Certainly, we have seen, the ability of American society to

---

25. Daryl Bem, *Beliefs, Attitudes and Human Affairs* (Belmont, California: Brooks/Cole Publishing Co., 1970), p. 89.
26. Ibid.

inculcate negative ideology concerning the Native American group has gone virtually unchallenged.

Bem goes on to apply this concept to stereotypes of women in our society, indicating the extent to which all social sources communicate the idea not only that women are "different" through some mysterious natural law, but that their only route to happiness and self-fulfillment lies in marriage, children, and "doing for" others. One point which Bem raises in this regard, pertinent to our discussion of racial attitudes, is that it is not only men who come to believe these things about women through continuous exposure to the stereotypes, but *women*, too, come to believe them.[27] Thus we should not be surprised to find Native Americans, raised in the midst of a white-controlled society, exposed to white education and white media (that is, institutional racism), who assimilate the non-conscious ideology of white supremacy. It is important to note that the cornerstone of nonconscious ideology is the *consistency* with which the messages are conveyed by all of the individual's reference groups, and that a dissident reference group can drive a wedge into this consistency, which leads the individual to question the accuracy of the ideology. This can help us understand those Native Americans who do not come to accept the nonconscious ideology of white superiority. If one is a member of a subculture which is strong enough to laud its own values over those of the whites, if one's parents emphasize the traditional ways, or if one is a member of a peer group which stresses Native Americanism, a wedge is driven into the consistency of nonconscious ideology, and it becomes possible to reject the image of one's group which has been propagated by many white-controlled reference groups.

The Principle of Constancy

The works of Jean Piaget and, more recently, of Lawrence Kohlberg, have made social scientists aware of the role that

---

27. Ibid., p. 99.

the child's own powers of cognition play in socialization, and in the world-view that the child holds at any given time.[28] Children proceed through stages of cognitive development, progressively mastering more and more sophisticated intellectual operations.

Most of the children we interviewed, and most of the children that other researchers of preschoolers' racial attitudes have studied, are in the stage of development which Piaget has designated as the "preoperational."[29] One of the characteristics that distinguishes the child of that age from the child of seven to thirteen (the stage of concrete operations) is that the younger child has not yet mastered the principle of constancy. Thus, while an older child will understand that water poured from a tall, skinny glass into a short, fat glass is still the same amount of water, the preoperational child will not understand this, and will believe that there is less water than there was before.

Kohlberg has applied this concept to sexual identity, indicating that young children may believe that they can turn into a member of the opposite sex by altering their hairstyle or dress. Kohlberg states that by five or six children settle on a sexual identity and see it as constant and unchangeable.[30] Thus, he implies that constancy in this area is acquired somewhat earlier than in the perception of weight and volume, which Piaget sees occurring after seven.

Erlich has suggested that this concept could be applied to racial identity as well, with preschool children believing that they are able to change racial identity.[31] This might explain a

28. Jean Piaget, *Psychology of Intelligence* (Totowa, N.J.: Littlefield, Adams & Co., 1973); and Lawrence Kohlberg, "A Cognitive-Developmental Analysis of Children's Sex-Role Concepts and Attitudes," in *The Development of Sex Differences,* ed. by Eleanor E. Macoby (Stanford: Stanford University Press, 1966), p. 164.

29. Piaget, *Psychology of Intelligence.*

30. Kohlberg, "Cognitive-Developmental Analysis," p. 95.

31. Howard J. Erlich, *The Social Psychology of Prejudice* (New York: John Wiley's Sons, 1973), p. 113.

good deal of the racial misidentification which has been noted in preschool minority-group children, and the fact that, after seven, this tendency fades and disappears. However, it cannot explain why more minority than white children misidentify. That can only be understood in terms of the positive imagery the society associates with white and the negative imagery which is associated with minority-group status. Thus, misidentification at the preschool level is probably a combination of cognitive and attitudinal factors.

It is my belief that there is a good deal to this suggestion, for, during the research, we did overhear several conversations in which children expressed the idea that a change in race was possible. One white child told me that she was "going to grow up into a Indian," and several Native American youngsters stated that they intended to become white in the future.

Associatedness

Another cognitive characteristic of young children is that which I shall call associatedness. This term refers to the child's tendency to combine two factors which are unrelated from the adult, logical point of view. This combining occurs in instances where, in the child's experience, when he has observed one of these characteristics, the other has also been present, and he has gained the idea that they go together all the time. Mothers know that red glass is a potential danger to a child who has been given red hard-candies. Redness, hardness, and transparency are associated in that child's mind with sweetness. To apply this concept more directly to our own subject matter, let us consider Tim, a four-year-old boy observed by the author for several months.

Tim lived in an upper-middle-class, all-white neighborhood and attended an all-white private nursery school. His parents were completely apolitical, and the civil rights struggle was never discussed in the home. His contact with minority-group people was nonexistent, with one exception. This exception was a very important person in his life. Her name was Mrs. B., a seventy-year-old black woman who spent a good deal of time with Tim. Mrs. B. had been his father's nurse, and had maintained close contact with the family; at least once a week, she came to visit Tim and play with him. Sometimes, if the parents were going to be away overnight, they would ask Mrs. B. to stay with Tim, preferring her to a babysitter. There was mutual affection between Tim and Mrs. B. However, Mrs. B. was concerned with her increasing years and spoke of this quite frequently. She verbalized her discontent with the limitations of old age and sometimes excused herself from Tim's games because of her age.

The winter of Tim's fourth year, his best friend, John, went to Florida on vacation for a month. Tim missed John and waited eagerly for his return. The day that John returned, Tim ran over to his house, but returned to his own home almost immediately, very saddened. "I can't play with John any more!" he sobbed to his astonished mother. "He came back *all old!*"

Of course, what had happened was that John had come back *brown,* but in Tim's mind brownness and oldness were synonymous. His only experience with brownness had been with old age, and he had only that experience to draw upon in interpreting his friend's changed appearance. No other external source of information had presented itself to disabuse him of this belief that brownness = agedness.

The story of Tim is especially relevant to us because to some extent it combines all of the concepts I have introduced in this chapter.

1. *Institutional racism.* This had prevented the child from encountering blacks who were not old. There were no black peers in his school, no black middle-aged people in his neighborhood, no pictures of blacks in his picture books, and none on television (this was pre-Sesame Street). His family knew only Mrs. B, and that was an employer-employee relationship.
2. *Nonconscious ideology.* All of the above factors, plus the

absence of any parental instruction on racial matters, had communicated to Tim the ideology of brown people as old and unable to be playful.

3. *Constancy.* Tim believed that John had changed races— and, for that matter, ages; that is, he saw such change as possible.

4. *Associatedness.* As his only experience with brownness had been with old age, he associated the two in his mind.[32]

It is not only the white child who makes such connections. That some confusion exists in the mind of the young minority-group child between race and other social characteristics he or she may have experienced in conjunction with race is brilliantly exemplified by Oscar Zeta Acosta's description of his own six-year-old's-eye view of his home town, Riverbank, California.

> Riverbank is divided into three parts, and in my corner of the world there were only three kinds of people: Mexicans, Okies and Americans. Catholics, Holy Rollers and Protestants. Peach pickers, cannery workers and clerks.[33]

To the small child, brown skin in Riverbank was synonymous with a certain occupation, a certain religion, and, Acosta also points out in his book, residence. It is only later that he comes to realize that these are not inexorably bound together.

I believe that these four concepts can help us understand the findings of our research with Native American children, and perhaps shed additional light on studies of the formation of children's racial attitudes.

---

32. There may be "double associatedness" here, too. Tim had shown a good deal if interest in the family's apple tree. He had been told not to eat the green apples because "they aren't old enough," had been allowed to eat red apples, and then had observed the apples turning brown. He may thus have made an association between what happens to fruit and what (as he saw it) happens to people.

33. Oscar Zeta Acosta, *The Autobiography of a Brown Buffalo* (New York: Bantam, 1972).

Interpreting the Data on Children's Racial Attitudes

We have seen that Native American children select white dolls for the positive stereotypes in the story and that a good many of them also select the white doll for a self-image. We have examined the explanations other researchers have given for similar findings with other minority-group youngsters. Let us now try to examine the way in which the concepts introduced in this chapter, in conjunction with some of the elements of more established theoretical interpretations of these data, can help us understand the formation of racial attitudes.

First, let us try to isolate the major findings which are consistent in the data, that is, trends which appear in many of the studies of preschool children's racial attitudes, including the children we have observed in this research. Then, let us consider the implications the four concepts introduced above have for these findings and, at the same time, how they can broaden our understanding of the research findings and resolve some of the apparent contradictions.

General Findings in the Field of Children's Racial Attitudes

The following general statements can be made about the attitudes of preschool and school-age youngsters, when we consider the research in this area as a whole. These statements are made with reference to the past research discussed above as well as the data at hand. This means that, basically, we are considering the work of the Clarks, Mary Ellen Goodman, Judith Porter, Hraba and Grant, Gregor and McPherson, and Bernard Rosenthal.[34] However, the treatment of theoretical

34. Clark and Clark, "Development of Consciousness" and "Racial Identification"; Goodman, *Race Awareness*; Porter, *Black Child, White Child*; J. Hraba and C. Grant, "Black is Beautiful: A Re-examination of Racial Preference and Identification," *Journal of Personality and Social Psychology* 7 (1967): 216-21; Gregor and McPherson, "Racial Preference and Ego Identity"; and Rosenthal, "Self-Identification in Chippewa Indians."

explanations will also draw upon the writing of persons who have not themselves carried out this type of empirical research with small children, such as Coles, Erikson, and Dollard.[35]

1. Children below the age of seven, both white and minority, evince (a) a preference for white, as measured by association of white with positive stereotypes; and (b) a tendency to select white self-images.

2. Five- and six-year-olds show a stronger tendency in this direction than three- and four-year-olds.

3. However, the relationship between age and white preference is not linear, as older children (blacks around age seven, Native Americans around age ten) reverse the tendency and show greater preference for their own race and identification with it.

4. While preference and self-identification are related to one another, there is little or no relationship between "awareness" of racial differences (such as the ability to match by color and to recognize racial terms) and either preference or self-identification. Thus, knowledge of color differences does not lead the five- or six-year-old to prefer his or her own race or to correct self-identification. In fact, as in the Native American case, the children most aware of these differences may identify all the more strongly with white.

5. This study indicates that while closer contact to the majority culture and exposure to face-to-face discrimination (as in the case of blacks or urban Native Americans) exacerbates the preference for white and the tendency to identify with it in preschool children, this condition is not *necessary* for children to form such attitudes. Even relatively isolated children have learned enough about the role allocation in our society and the status of their

35. Coles, *Children of Crisis*; Erik Erikson, "The Concept of Identity in Race Relations: Notes and Queries," *Daedalus* 95 (1966): 154-71; and Allison Davis and John Dollard, *Children of Bondage* (New York: Peter Smith, 1964).

racial groups to evince white preference and self-identification.

6. Children of preschool age seem to understand the roles occupied by the members of different races in American society, as is apparent in the spontaneous remarks made by the children in this study which are cited in the preceding chapter. Other studies which also have indicated this are the De Fleurs' study, which revealed the grasp children had of occupational roles, and Trager and Radke's study of doll dressing, in which children assigned the dress associated with menial roles to black dolls.[36]

These findings, especially those which have found a preference for white in minority children and a tendency to identify with it, have been taken by the mark of oppression school as evidence of severe psychological damage to children, caused by the influence of minority-group status on personality. The identification with white is viewed as an escape into fantasy to avoid the reality of racial status, the minority-group child imagining himself or herself to be white. The fact that older children do not do this is explained as a bitter acceptance of reality. However, this school of thought can offer no real explanation for the reversal (or "acceptance") and its occurrence at age seven rather than at any other age, except the child's loss of imaginativeness and ability to fantasize, culminating in an acceptance of reality.

Nor does this theory differentiate between the perception of the roles held by members of racial groups in the society as unpleasant or oppressed, and personal self-hatred. Yet, Porter has pointed out that the concepts of racial identification and personal self-esteem are separate dimensions of personality. I would add that racial identification, and the realization that

36. DeFleur and DeFleur, "The Relative Contribution of Television," pp. 777-89; Helen Trager and Marion Radke, "Children's Perceptions of Social Roles of Negroes and Whites," *Journal of Psychology* 29 (1950): 3-33.

the allocation of roles in the society is a factor of race, are also two separate psychological realities.

Further, I contend that the realization that role allocation and the value of racial membership are separate factors is not a function of deep-lying psychological factors, but is a function of the cognitive development of the child. At different stages in his or her life, the ability to organize information received from the environment differs according to the sophistication of the child's intelligence. In addition to this, we must keep in mind that institutional racism and nonconscious ideology may limit the materials with which the child's intelligence will be permitted to work. By keeping all of these factors in mind, we can get an overall picture of what stages the child will go through in the formation of attitudes about his or her racial group.

At three or four, children are exposed to few persons outside their primary group. Parents, siblings, and grandparents, and perhaps an occasional babysitter, make up the circle of persons with whom he or she has contact. Even if the circle is larger, the cognitive makeup of the child does not permit it to take much interest in larger social units; rather, children of this age concentrate on significant others and the roles those others play in their own lives. Like the people of long ago who believed that the sun revolved about the earth, at this stage, the small person sees society and those who populate it mainly in terms of their function vis-à-vis himself or herself. This limitation of the circle of others is certainly true for the small Native American, who stays close to home and mother or grandmother.

However, at five and six, with a better grasp of language and locomotion and a firmer knowledge of how the world works, the child's world begins to enlarge. He or she takes part in new activities, begins to have access to books, and has the newly acquired attention span to *watch* television (rather than play with the television on). School also means filling public-health requirements and the encounter with the medical establishment for those children who had avoided it until this point in their lives. The child may begin to go more places with his or her parents, and while these things are happening, the child's mental abilities to perceive and to make sense of the social world are also maturing. The child is learning and understanding more and more all the time of the social map of the United States, and realizing that the life-styles of the people who inhabit this country, and the roles they are able to play, are in large part determined by race. Thus, this child shows more awareness of racial differences, more white preference, and more white identification than his or her younger counterpart. For, everywhere, whites seem to have better, more important positions, cleaner, newer clothes, bigger, prettier homes in which to live, and many fine belongings that only money can buy. In school, the teachers are white; at the clinic, the doctors are white; the man who rents father's land is white; most of the police and social workers are white; and of course, the "beautiful people," those whose faces grace the covers of magazines and the screens of television sets, are also white, and more than likely blond and blue-eyed.

Here the two cognitive concepts of constancy and associatedness enter to play important roles in the interpretation of the data. The five- and six-year-old has not yet fully mastered the principle of constancy. He or she may believe that it is really possible to change race. Thus, when offered a choice (and let us remember, it is the interviewer who acts as if it *were* a choice) of race, he or she may indicate the white doll. There are two important issues here.

The first is that viewing the choice this way is very different from regarding the choice as a fantasizing of the self as white. It is also a very different interpretation than that which sees this behavior as a rejection of racial status. As the child believes change to be possible and is, in addition, confronted by an adult who acts as if racial membership were indeed a choice, no deep-lying mechanism of denial seems to be at work. Rather, the child enters into the choosing situation with the belief that he or she *can* be the race he or she selects.

Second, this explanation places much more emphasis on (1)

social institutions, statuses, and roles, and (2) the child as an *active learner* of the social map. Most explanations of the formation of children's attitudes, as I noted, operate on the assumption that the child has learned about race through some sort of *experiences*. This has the effect of making it appear that the absence of harmful racial incidents in a child's life would render the child free of an unfavorable view of his or her own race. It also sees the child as a passive receptacle into whom knowledge is being poured by external agents—as a *reactor* to rewarding or punishing situations rather than as an active participant in his or her own life. Yet we must consider the child as actor/learner to fully comprehend the development of racial attitudes. Regarding the child as actor/learner of sex roles, Kohlberg writes:

> Regardless of ultimate findings in parent-child sex-role correlates, the specificity of the correlations already established indicates that very generalized reinforcement and identification mechanisms do not in themselves provide an adequate explanation for the development of sex-role attitudes in children. These correlations become intelligible only when we interpret them in terms of the common or "natural" sex-role concepts, values and identifications of children of a given age and sex. The development of these concepts and values, however, can be explained in terms of basic cognitive-developmental trends and processes.[37]

The same could be said of racial roles. The child does not learn about racial status through reward and punishment, or, necessarily, through parental instruction, but rather *observes* racial differences in an attempt to organize the world and to incorporate in his or her mind his or her own body image in its many aspects. The child's mind is the mill; institutional racism and nonconscious ideology determine and limit the grist.

To illustrate the independent role of the child's cognition in the acquisition of racial attitudes, let us consider the career

37. Kohlberg, "Cognitive-Development Analysis."

choice of a young friend, aged five. Dick is a handsome young black man, the child of adoptive white middle-class parents. The parents were active in the Civil Rights movement and had arranged Dick's life so that he would be in nonracist situations. They had moved to a primarily black neighborhood, and placed Dick in a progressive, integrated nursery school. Whenever Dick showed a talent or ability, it was encouraged, and he was constantly praised and told that he could be whatever he wanted as an adult. Yet, one day Dick came home and announced that, when he grew up, he would become a garbage man. The parents in good humor said that was a fine idea, and the father said it sounded so fine, he might become a garbage man also. "No, Daddy, you can't be one," responded Dick. "You're *white*." This child, who had received all the positive *teaching* that a family could give, had nonetheless done his own *observing and learning*.

Alvin Poussaint of Harvard University also stresses the child as observer:

> A child's sense of self is affected by how he views his environment both through direct involvement and through various media presentations. The powerful influence of television and films often challenges parental guidance. Even a child in a strong family may develop self-doubt if he lives in the midst of poverty and social disorder. A poor young Black viewing television may see no representatives of his community or lifestyle and get the impression that he does not count in this society. He may decide that "worthwhile" people live in the middle-class homes and neighborhoods he sees in television commercials.[38]

A cognitive approach can also help us explain the switch to the more positive attitudes in children which researchers have observed in older subjects, eight to ten years of age. The older child has a better grasp of the institutional arrangements in society but in addition has made two cognitive advances which are of relevance here. One is that the older child has

38. Poussaint, "Building a Strong Self-Image."

mastered the principle of constancy. That is, he or she knows that race, like size and volume, is not changeable. Therefore, in measures of self-identification, the child confronts the testing situation itself with less flexibility. No longer does he or she believe that one can change one's race. Rather, one is brown, black, or white, just as one is either a boy or a girl, and there are no two ways about it. Therefore, choices become more "realistic" from the adult point of view.

The other new cognitive ability of the older child is the beginning of categorization, or the ability to find exclusive and nonoverlapping ways of classifying social objects. It is this ability that leads the older child to move away from the "associatedness" described above. This is the stage when Oscar Zeta Acosta realized that there were white Catholics, the stage when the black child may realize that there are white garbage men, and black doctors and judges. In other words, it is the stage at which characteristics which at first seemed to be always bound together, such as Acosta's brown–Mexican–peach-picking–Catholic characteristics, are recognized as logically separate dimensions of identity.

The implications of this development for a consideration of tests of minority-group children's racial attitudes lie in this ability to separate out social factors which previously were regarded as inseparable. Once the child realizes that color and occupation, or color and residence, or color and type of clothing, are not necessarily synonymous, he or she does not have to select a white self-image to proclaim a desire for such social rewards as wealth, health, and stylish clothing. For the younger child, race was so bound up with other factors that to identify with "the good life" necessitated, to some extent, an identification with whiteness. The older child is able to split these dimensions and mentally conceive of his or her own race as logically compatible with the desired goals.

There is a certain irony in this, in that the realities of institutional racism have been such (and still are, to a somewhat lesser extent) that the younger, cognitively less-developed child's perception was probably a more accurate appraisal of his or her real life-chances. That is, color and occupation, color and prestige, or color and health are highly correlated in our society—not intrinsically, but because of racial restrictions that extend back many generations. These restrictions made it impossible for all but a token few minority persons to attain middle-class status and/or prestigious occupations. In the Native American case, these restrictions almost prevented survival itself.

A cognitive-learning approach is also essential for explaining the white preference of isolated minority children, such as the reservation children in our sample. If children learned about the position of their race only through experience and instruction, there would be little reason for reservation children to evince a preference for white, as they have had very little contact with whites, especially children of their own ages, and have not experienced discrimination in school and play. However, they do observe the social system in which they find themselves. They see it at work in a variety of ways which I have described. Thus, they come to perceive and understand the positions that Native Americans hold in this system as very low on the United States pecking order. This, and not racial self-hatred, is what their answers and spontaneous remarks reveal to us. These children do not see whites as naturally better people, but rather, they see white skin as inextricably associated with "the good life."

Our emphasis on cognitive learning should not be interpreted as a statement that parental instruction and experience do not influence the development of children's racial attitudes. Of course these factors play a vital role. The point here is that those factors alone are not sufficient to explain the formation of these attitudes, because the cognition of the child plays its own independent role in the acquisition of racial attitudes. (An illustrative mapping of the theory is presented in table 14.) The main contention of this book is that institutional racism and the propagation of nonconscious ideologies concerning a

Table 14

Age of child and presence or absence of the factors associated with perceptions of racial dimensions of social life

Age	Perception of Institutional Racism; Understanding of Racial Hierarchies	Absorption of Non-conscious Ideology	Under-standing of Constancy of Racial Status	Association of Race with Other Unrelated Traits
3 & 4	Little awareness.	Some exposure from television, but limited absorption.	No	Yes
5 & 6	Exposure increased through broadening of social experience; perceives hierarchy.	Peak time for absorbing messages the culture conveys.	No	Yes
7 to 10	Exposure levels off, understands societal arrangements and racial hierarchy.	Absorbs a good deal, but peers and activist parents can drive a wedge in the consistency of the ideology through counter-ideology.	Yes	No

group in the general culture are sufficient conditions for the acquisition of an attitude of white superiority on the part of children of all races. Parental instruction consistent with the messages of the racial ideologies can only exacerbate these attitudes. On the other hand, parental training which contradicts them can play a vital role in establishing positive racial attitudes in children. This is especially true for the minority-group parent. Our data with the children of activists suggest that a home in which the positive value of Native American-ness is stressed will produce children who feel positive about their group. Dr. Poussaint also suggests that black parents take an active role in discounting the portrait of blacks conveyed by the white structural and cultural systems:

> Black parents must expose their children to the positive side of their heritage. Black children should be given a sense of history. . . .A strong racial identity will lapse if children are not taught about their heritage.[39]

Certainly all of what Dr. Poussaint has to say could be applied to Native American children as well. Parents must take deliberate and positive steps to offset the influence of institutional racism on their children's sense of racial identity. Thus cognitive learning theory can explain findings in this area in what I believe to be a more effective and common sense manner than the explanations offered by the mark of oppression school.

All of the above indicates as well that the color-blind school is extremely limited and, to a large extent, incorrect in its interpretation of data concerning the racial attitudes of small children. This can, in part, be explained by the fact that many of these theorists have worked primarily with older children and adults, which has not really exposed them to the definite preference for whiteness and identification with it that exist in preschoolers. As Porter has suggested, this school of thought

39. Ibid.

is certainly adequate in its ability to assess findings about personal self-worth, but not in explaining feelings about the self as a minority-group member. Also, in limiting itself to the concept of individual self-worth, this school of thought limits its concept of damage to personality. In this interpretation, "damage" comes to mean only mental illness, psychological debilitation, or crushed self-esteem. Yet, I would contend that it is "damaging" for the minority-group child to be confronted with a social reality that leads him or her to the belief that there is a correlation between his or her color and the ability to succeed in society. Age, and, with it, further cognitive development, will help the child separate these dimensions from one another, but the separation will be very difficult if there are no examples for the child to observe which contradict the correlation. The child may come, indeed, to realize that brownness need not always be associated with poverty, nor blackness with poor housing, but this is dependent on the extent of institutional racism and the consistency of nonconscious racial ideology conveyors. Even in the best of situations, the younger child has been influenced by the preschool association between race and life-style, which can cause that child undue unhappiness and can lead to the development, at preschool age, of defense mechanisms and behavior patterns which may be difficult or impossible to jettison at a later stage in the life cycle, when cognition is conveying a more optimistic message.

The color-blind school allows whites and white institutions to escape the consequences of existing social structural arrangements by implying that only family experiences—interactions with the child's significant others—can cause personality damage, and that race is only a variable contributing to family relations. In this view only minority parents can be seen as damaging the personalities of minority-group children. Thus, the causes come to be rooted in the minority primary group, and the proposed "cures" have to do with psychoanalysis of adults and the "strengthening" of the minority family. This is patent nonsense. If the "cause" lies in children's perception of social roles, the "cure" lies in changing social institutions.

Summary

This chapter has interpreted the findings of our study of Native American youngsters and other findings in the field of the development of children's racial attitudes in light of four concepts: institutional racism, nonconscious ideology, the principle of constancy, and associatedness. I have contended that these concepts help us offer a more adequate explanation of the findings than those offered by the mark of oppression or the color-blind schools of thought.

This combination of the four concepts can be put in the form of a third interpretation of the data, which, together with some of the elements of the other two interpretations, explains the tendency of preschool children to show white preference and a tendency to identify the self as white. This explanation also helps to explain why these tendencies tend to fade in the older child. (Table 15 compares the three interpretations.)

Simply restated, this third interpretation places emphasis on the child as a cognitive actor, one who is learning about the social world he or she inhabits and trying to make sense of it. The preschool child, from late four to six years of age, is increasingly exposed to larger social units and to the major social institutions, both first hand (as in visits to the doctor) and vicariously (through television). Given the racial polarization of American society and the distortion of role allocation which has resulted from generations of racism and discrimination, the world that presents itself to the child is characterized by white dominance and the oppression of brown, black, and red people. The child perceives this and realizes that white is a status which is more likely to bring with it the good things of life. In addition, the smaller child (four to six) has not yet grasped the principle of constancy and may believe that it is really possible to change race and to become white, or brown. The child of this age also tends to associate two or more dimensions of social existence under one rubric. Thus, brown and poor, although logically separate dimensions of life, may appear to come in a single package, from the five-year-old point of view.

Table 15

Interpretations of the influence of life in white society on the
minority-group child and their implications for solutions

Interpretation	Influence of Minority-Group Membership on Personality	Solutions
Color Blind	Only influence on personality is that of primary group, especially parent-child interaction. Race seen as important only indirectly' as in its influence on family structure and interaction.	Psychoanalysis if a problem exists. "Strengthening" of minority family structure.
Mark of Oppression	Child internalizes the low esteem in which the larger society holds his or her race, self-hatred and rejection of own race take place.	Changing white attitudes. Prompt handling of racial slurs.
Institutional Racism-Cognition	Child, through observation, learns roles played in society by his or her own race. Sees that these are either inferior or devalued. Sees that life styles resulting from this role allocation are different for the different races. Wants the same life options as whites.	Cultural revolution: Black is beautiful. Structural revolution: role re-allocation on a major scale.

Later, children learn the constancy of racial membership and, in addition, lose the tendency to associate logically unassociated traits. Thus, they can realize that their racial membership is not synonymous with other social characteristics, such as poverty and ill health.

The fact that reservation youngsters are as likely to go through these inner experiences as blacks certainly indicates the powerful influence of institutional racism as a shaper of children's attitudes, apart from any influence that actual face-to-face encounters with bigoted whites may have.

Some Closing Thoughts On Policy Implications

In the past several years, our solutions to the problem of low racial self-esteem in minority children have been directed by the theory that the suffering of outright personal discrimination causes damage to the self-esteem of minority-group children. Thus, it is assumed that if white attitudes get better (as indeed Pettigrew has indicated they have[40]), fewer minority children will suffer such incidents, and all will be well. In addition, the "Black is beautiful" movement has aimed at increasing the pride of black youngsters in their own appearance and in their cultural heritage.

Two other trends, the ghettoization of the cities and the ideology of black separatism, have created islands of blackness in white society—islands which are protective in part. The children on these islands are surrounded by other blacks, attend school with other blacks, and play with other blacks. They are protected to a large extent from those hurting incidents to which I have referred. This description of the lives of black youngsters may sound similar to the description of the lives of Native American reservation children. That is because the two situations are coming to resemble each other more and more.

40. Thomas Pettigrew, *Racially Separate or Together?* (New York: McGraw-Hill, 1971), pp. 165-203.

We must remember, however, that the reservation children in the study showed low own-race preference and low racial self-identification. This indicates that cultural insulation is not enough. One cannot easily deceive children. They are perceptive little creatures who are busily assembling the picture-puzzle of the social world. An all-Native American play group does not prevent the child's realization that all the important people on television are white, or that the BIA officials who exert control over his parents and their friends are white. Similarly, the cry of "Black is beautiful" cannot blind the black child to white power and black powerlessness in the economic and political worlds.

We must begin to turn our efforts to combating institutional racism—to altering the role structure of society that our children are absorbing. The way to develop positive attitudes towards his or her own race in the minority-group child is to provide that child with a view of society in which the hierarchy of power is not correlated with race. When the minority-group child perceives a world where his or her people are well represented in all roles, especially those which bring with them respect and self-determination, as well as a diminishing of prejudice, we will find minority-group children who truly value their racial membership and actively identify with it.

APPENDIX

The Story

———◆◆———

The first story we're going to tell is about a school (to school child). Does this room look a little bit like your school room? (To child at home) Do you go to school? Well, this is a room in a school. Maybe it's like the room in your school (or the "school where you will go," to child who hasn't yet gone to nursery or day care school). A little boy (or girl—same sex as child) goes to this school. This little boy is named John (Mary) and he looks just exactly like you. (The interviewer brings out a matched pair of dolls of child's own sex and shows them to child.) Which one of these boys shall we have be John in our story? *Which one looks just like you?* (Through our description of the test from this point on, the italicized sentences will indicate a "doll-choice point" in the narrative. As the child indicates his choice, the interviewer removes the rejected doll from view.)

OK. You may hold John. Do you want to put him in this school? OK. John likes his school because he has fun playing there, and sometimes he gets things to eat. (This reference to food at school was added to the Porter test to help the Native American children identify with the situation more intensely. Breakfast and lunch are important parts of most Indian preschool programs and are popular events in the daily lives of the children.) It looks like John got to school early in the morning today. He's the only one in school. He's waiting for someone. Do you know who he's waiting for? Well, he's waiting for his best friend. *One of these boys is John's best friend that he plays with all the time. Which one is John's best friend?* (The darker doll is held in opposite hand from the first selection now to prevent a "response set" on the part of the subject, which might occur if the darker doll were always on the left or the right.) All right. You take John's friend and put him with John. They are playing together with trucks (dolls) when some girls come in, and John says, "One of these girls is really nice. Let's ask her to play with us." *Which girl does John think is very nice?* OK. Let's put her in the school, too. All the children are playing together, and some more kids come in, so John says to his friend: "Hey, let's ask them to play, too!" But John's friend says, "Nah—I don't like one of those girls—*she's lazy and stupid.* I don't want to play with her!" *Which one of these girls does John's friend think is lazy and stupid?* What about John? What does he say? Does he agree with his friend? Well, the kids all play and have such a good time that, before they know it, it's time to go home. John remembers that Mommy said he could bring a friend home with him for lunch. *Which one of these children should John take home for lunch? Why does he want to take that one?* (Indicate rejected doll.) *What would Mommy say if he brought this one home, too? Would she like it?* (If "no"—why not?) That was fun, wasn't it? (Fortunately none of them ever said "No"!)

Would you like to tell another story? This story is about a house. (Sets are reversed so child is facing house and school is facing away from him.) Do you know who lives in this house? A boy (girl) named Bob (Mary) lives here, and Bob is a boy who looks just like you. *Which one do you want to be Bob in our story?* OK. Why don't you help me by putting Bob in the house? This is a very special day to Bob. Can you guess why? Well, it's his birthday. Do you like birthdays? Me, too! Bob's father is here today. (The statement is phrased in this way because some children come from father-absent homes. However, most fathers take an interest in the child's welfare, and it seemed quite natural to expect father to show up on a special day. The children from father-present homes were not puzzled by the statement as they interpreted it as, "Father is staying home today.") *One of these men is Bob's father. Which one do you want to be Bob's father in the story?* OK. Bob and his father are talking about Bob's birthday, and Father says he thinks people will come and bring presents for Bob.

(Note this is slightly different from the "birthday party" story used by Porter. While doll-choice questions are phrased to tap the same affective dimensions as in the Porter study, the story is slightly different in two respects. First, a party as such is not always part of the Native American child's birthday. Second, when celebrations do take place, they are not attended by the peer group exclusively, but by people of all generations. The Native American child lives much more in a world of several generations than his white counterpart. Therefore, more adult roles were added to the story.)

Just when Father was saying that, there was a knock at the door, and two men were there. They brought things for Bob. What do you think they brought him?

Father tells Bob he is especially glad to see one of the men. He likes this man very much, and they are best friends. *Which one is Father's best friend?* OK. You can hold Father's friend. Then Mother comes in. *Which one of these women is Bob's mother?* Bob hears another knock at the door, and there are two girls from his school with presents for him. Mother hasn't met these girls so she goes to meet them, and she says to Bob: "Oh, Bob! One of these girls looks so pretty and neat!" *Which girl does Mother think looks so pretty and neat?* Then Bob opens his presents and Mother brings out some cake and soda pop. Some women came to the house then, and they say,

"Happy Birthday, Bob!" Mother goes to greet them and offers them some cake and soda pop. "Oh, dear!" she says to Bob. "I have only one soda pop left. Which lady should I give the soda pop to?" What does Bob say? Which lady does he want Mother to give the soda pop to? Well, the men want to take the kids outside to play games, so all the men are outside and all the women are inside. (In the house the interviewer lines up four women—white flowered dress, Native American red dress, white red dress, Native American flowered dress.) Which of these ladies look alike or the same? (Child has a chance here to match by dress or race.) Then two of the mothers go out (flowered white and red-dressed Native American are removed), and two of the men come in. (Native American in coat and tie, white in shirt sleeves are put in house.) Which of these people look alike? (Child here can choose by sex or race; all are dressed differently, so child cannot choose by dress.)

(The child can then play freely. After awhile the interviewer picks up the Native American father doll and places it on the "sofa" and holds up a pair of women dolls matched in dress for the child to see.) Which of these women is that man's wife? Which one is in his family?

OK. They are a mother and a father. Now, let's give them a boy for their family. Which one of these boys is their little boy? There is a girl in the family, too. Which one of these girls belongs to that family?

This process is repeated using a white father to "start" the family. At the end of the test, while putting dolls away, the researcher holds up the four "Mother" dolls and asks, "Do any of these women look like Indian women?"

As some Native American children know their tribal name, as well as or instead of the generic term "Indian," we repeated this question substituting the tribal name instead of "Indian." The question was repeated using the "Father" dolls.

At the end of the interview, the child was thanked for his or her participation and given a small present, such as a box of crayons or a jack ball.

Bibliography

Ablon, Joan. "Relocated American Indians in the San Francisco Bay Area: Social Interaction and Indian Identity." *Human Organization* 23 (1964): 296–304.

Acosta, Oscar Zeta. *The Autobiography of a Brown Buffalo.* New York: Bantam, 1972.

Adorno, T. W., Brunswick Frenkel, Daniel Levinson, and R. Sanford. *The Authoritarian Personality.* New York: Harper and Brothers, 1950.

Akwesasne Notes 3, no. 8. (December 1969).

Allport, Gordon. *The Nature of Prejudice.* Garden City, N.Y.: Doubleday Anchor Books, 1958.

Ammons, R. B. "Reactions in a Projective Doll Play Interview of White Males Two to Six Years Old to Differences in

Skin Color and Facial Features." *Journal of Genetic Psychology* 76 (1950): 323–41.

Anderson, James G., and Dwight Safar. "The Influence of Differential Community Perceptions on the Provision of Equal Educational Opportunities." In *Native Americans Today*, edited by Bahr, Chadwick, and Day. New York: Harper and Row, 1972. Pp. 69–79.

Asher, Steven, and Vernon Allen. "Racial Preference and Social Comparison Processes." *Journal of Social Issues* 25 (1969): 157–66.

Asubel, David. "Ego Development Among Segregated Negro Children." In *Mental Health and Segregation*, edited by Martin Grossack. New York: Springer Publishing Company, 1963. Pp. 33–40.

Bahr, Howard. "An End to Invisibility." In *Native Americans Today*, edited by Bahr, Chadwick, and Day. New York: Harper and Row, 1972. Pp. 404–12.

Bahr, Howard, Bruce A. Chadwick, and Robert C. Day, eds. *Native Americans Today: Sociological Perspectives.* New York: Harper and Row, 1972.

Barnouw, B. Victor. "Acculturation and Personality Change Among the Wisconsin Chippewa." *American Anthropological Memoir,* no. 72 (1950): 152.

Baughman, Earl, and Grant Dahlstrom. *Negro and White Children: A Psychological Study in the Rural South.* New York: Academic Press, 1968.

Bem, Daryl J. *Beliefs, Attitudes and Human Affairs.* Belmont, Calif.: Brooks/Cole Publishing Co., 1970.

Bigart, Homer. "Militancy of Urban Indians Spurs Hope for Change." *New York Times,* 10 February 1972, p. 1.

Bird, Charles, Elio Monschesi, and Harvey Burdick. "Studies of Group Tensions III. The Effect of Parental Discouragement of Play Activities Upon the Attitudes of White Children Towards Negroes." *Child Development* 23 (1952): 295–306.

Blake, Robert, and Wayne Dennis. "Development of Stereotypes Concerning the Negro." *Journal of Abnormal and Social Psychology* 38 (1943): 525–31.

Blalock, Hubert M., Jr. *Social Statistics.* New York: McGraw Hill, 1960.

Boggs, S. T. "An Interactional Study of Ojibwa Socialization." *American Sociological Review* 21 (1956): 191.

———. "Cultural Change and the Personality of Ojibwa Children." *American Anthropologist* 60 (1958): 47–58.

Bogardus, Emory. "Changes in Racial Distance." *International Journal of Attitude and Opinion Research* 1 (1947): 55–62.

———. "Measuring Social Distance." *Sociology and Social Research* 9 (1925): 299–308.

———. "Racial Distance." In *Sociological Analysis: An Empirical Approach through Replication,* edited by Murray A. Straus and Joel I. Nelson. New York: Harper and Row, 1968. Pp. 276–81.

Bongartz, Roy. "The New Indian." In *Native Americans Today,* edited by Bahr, Chadwick, and Day. New York: Harper and Row, 1972. Pp. 490–98.

Bowker, Lee H. "Red and Black in Contemporary American History Texts: A Content Analysis." In *Native Americans Today,* edited by Bahr, Chadwick, and Day. New York: Harper and Row, 1972. Pp. 101–9.

Brenman, Margaret. "Urban Lower Class Negro Girls." In *Mental Health and Segregation,* edited by Martin Grossack. New York: Springer Publishing Co., 1963. Pp. 83–108.

Brink, William, and Louis Harris. *Black and White.* New York: Simon and Schuster, 1967.

Brook, R. "What Tribe? Whose Island?" *North American Review* 7 (1970): 51–56.

Burgess, Elaine. "Poverty and Dependency: Some Selected Characteristics." *Journal of Social Issues* 21 (1965): 83–85.

Burnett, Robert, and John Koster. *The Road to Wounded Knee.* New York: Bantam Books, 1974.

Bushnell, John H. "From American Indian to Indian American: The Changing Identity of the Hupa." In *Native Americans Today,* edited by Bahr, Chadwick, and Day. New York: Harper and Row, 1972. Pp. 249–61.

Bynum, Jack. "Suicide and the American Indian: An Analysis

of Recent Trends." In *Native Americans Today,* edited by
Bahr, Chadwick, and Day. New York: Harper and Row,
1972. Pp. 367–77.

Cahn, Edgar, ed. *Our Brother's Keeper: The Indian in White
America.* Washington: New Community Press, 1969.

Campbell, Angus, and Howard Schuman. "Racial Attitudes in
Fifteen American Cities." In *Supplemental Studies for the
National Advisory Council on Civil Disorders.* Washing-
ton, D.C.: Government Printing Office, 1968. Pp. 1–68.

Campbell, Barbara. "Young Crees in Montana Educated From
an Indian's Point of View." *New York Times,* 1 January 1972, p. 21.

Castetter, Edward F., and Willis H. Bell. *Pima and Papago
Indian Agriculture.* Albuquerque, N.M.: University of New
Mexico Press, 1942.

Chadwick, Bruce A. "The Inedible Feast." In *Native Americans Today,* edited by Bahr, Chadwick, and Day. New
York: Harper and Row, 1972. Pp. 131–45.

Clark, Kenneth. *Prejudice and Your Child.* Boston: Beacon
Press, 1955. 2d ed., enl., 1963.

Clark, Kenneth, and Mamie Clark. "The Development of Consciousness of Self and the Emergence of Racial Identity in
Negro Pre-School Children." *Journal of Social Psychology*
10 (1939): 591–99.

———. "Emotional Factors in Racial Identification and Preference in Negro Children." In *Mental Health and Segregation,* edited by Martin Grossack. New York: Springer
Publishing Company, 1963. Pp. 53–63.

———. "Racial Identification and Preference in Negro Children."
In *Readings in Social Psychology,* edited by Eleanore
Maccoby and Newcomb T. Hartley. New York: Henry
Holt and Company, 1958. Pp. 602–11.

———. "Skin Color as a Factor in Racial Identification of Negro
Preschool Children." *Journal of Social Psychology* 11
(1940): 159–69.

Coleman, James S., Ernest Campbell, Carol Hobson, James
McPartland, Alexander Moot, Frederic Weinfeld, and

Robert York. *Equality of Educational Opportunity.* Washington, D.C.: Government Printing Office, 1966.

Coles, Robert. *Children of Crisis.* Boston: Little, Brown & Co., 1967.

Collier, Peter. "The Red Man's Burden." *Ramparts* 8 (February 1970): 26–38.

Comess, L. J., et al. "Congenital Anomalies and Diabetes in the Pima Indians of Arizona." *Diabetes* 18, no. 7 (1969): 471-77.

Committee on Interior and Insular Affairs. *Indian Health Care Improvement Act: Hearings Before the Subcommittee on Indian Affairs of the Committee on Interior and Insular Affairs United States Senate Ninety-Third Congress Second Session on S. 2938 To Implement the Federal Responsibility for the Care and Education of the Indian People by Improving the Services and Facilities of Federal Indian Health Programs and Encouraging Maximum Participation of Indians in Such Programs, and for Other Purposes.* Washington, D.C.: Government Printing Office, 1974.

Davis, Allison, and John Dollard. *Children of Bondage.* Washington: American Council on Education, 1940.

Dawes, H. L. "Have We Failed With the Indian?" *Atlantic* 84 (August 1899): 280–85.

Day, Robert C. "The Emergence of Activism as a Social Movement." In *Native Americans Today,* edited by Bahr, Chadwick, and Day. New York: Harper and Row, 1972. Pp. 506–31.

De Fleur, Melvin, and Lois B. De Fleur. "The Relative Contribution of Television As A Learning Source for Children's Occupational Knowledge." *American Sociological Review* 32 (1967): 777–89.

Deloria, Vine, Jr. *Custer Died For Your Sins: An Indian Manifesto.* New York: Avon Books, 1969.

———. "This Country Was a Lot Better Off When the Indians Were Running It." In *Native Americans Today,* edited by Bahr, Chadwick, and Day. New York: Harper and Row,

1972. Reprinted from *New York Times Magazine*, 8 March 1970.

———. *We Talk, You Listen: New Tribes, New Turf*. New York: Macmillan, 1970.

Deutsch, Martin. "Minority Group and Class Status as Related to Social and Personality Factors in Scholastic Achievement." In *Mental Health and Segregation*, edited by Martin Grossack. New York: Springer Publishing Co., 1963. Pp. 64–75.

Deutsch, Martin, et al. *The Disadvantaged Child*. New York: Basic Books, 1967.

———. "Guidelines for Testing Minority Group Children." Prepared by a work group for the Psychological Study of Social Issues. *Journal of Social Issues* 20 (1964): 129–45.

Dorsey, Rev. J. Owen. "Omaha Sociology." *Annual Report of the Bureau of Ethnology*. Washington: Government Printing Office, 1885. Pp. 205–370.

Dowling, J. H. "Rural Indian Community in an Urban Setting." *Human Organization* 27 (Fall 1968): 236–40.

Driver, Harold E. *Indians of North America*. 2d ed., rev. Chicago: University of Chicago Press, 1970.

———. "On the Population Nadir of Indians in the United States." *Cultural Anthropology* 9 (1968): 330.

Dumont, R. O., and Murray Wax. "Cherokee School Society and the Intercultural Classroom." *Human Organization* 28 (1969): 217–26.

Dunning, R. W. "Ethnic Relations and the Marginal Man in Canada." *Human Organization* 18 (1969): 117–22.

DuTort, B. "Substitution: A Process in Culture Change." *Human Organization* 23 (1964): 61–66.

Ellison, Ralph. *Shadow and Act*. New York: New American Library, 1966.

Erikson, Erik. *Childhood and Society*. 2d ed. New York: Norton and Company, 1963.

———. "The Concept of Identity in Race Relations." *Daedalus* 95 (1966): 145–71.

Erlich, Howard J. *The Social Psychology of Prejudice.* New York: John Wiley and Sons, 1973.

Ezell, P. H. "Is There a Hohokam-Pima Culture Continuum?" *American Antiquity* 29 (1963): 61–66.

Fauman, S. Joseph. "Status Crystallization and Interracial Attitudes." *Social Forces* 47 (1968): 53–60.

Ferguson, Frances N. "Navaho Drinking: Some Tentative Hypotheses." *Human Organization* 27 (1968): 159–67.

Fisher, A. D. "White Rites versus Indian Rights." In *Native Americans Today,* edited by Bahr, Chadwick, and Day. New York: Harper and Row, 1972. Pp. 155–61.

Fleischmann, Larry. "Richey School, Hope Symbol For Forgotten Vaqui Indians." *Arizona Daily Wildcat,* 9 February 1972, p. 12.

Fletcher, A. C., and Francis LaFlesche. "The Omaha Tribe." *Annual Reports of the Bureau of American Ethnology* XXVII. Washington, D.C.: Government Printing Office, 1906. Pp. 17–644.

Foreman, Grant. *Indian Removal: The Emigration of The Five Civilized Tribes of Indians.* New ed. Norman, Okla.: University of Oklahoma Press, 1953.

Fortune, R. F. *Omaha Secret Societies.* New York: Columbia University Press, 1932; printed in Germany.

Frantz, Joe. "The Frontier Tradition. An Invitation to Violence." In *The History of Violence in America,* edited by Hugh Davis Graham and Ted Robert Gurr. A report submitted to the National Commission on the Causes and Prevention of Violence. New York: Bantam Books, 1969.

Frenkel-Brunswick, Else, Daniel J. Levinson, and R. Nevitt Sanford. "A Study of Prejudice in Children." *Human Relations* 1 (1948): 295–306.

Fuchs, Estelle, and Robert Havighurst, *To Live on This Earth.* Garden City, N.Y.: Doubleday, 1972.

Gessell, Arnold Lucius, and Frances Lillian Ilg. *The Child From Five to Ten.* New York and London: Harper and Brothers, 1946.

Gitter, A., and Yoidi Satow. "Color and Physiognomy as Variables in Racial Misidentification Among Children." *Proceedings of 77th Annual Conference of American Psychological Association,* 1969.

Goldfrank, Florence I. "Historic Change and Social Character: A Study of the Teton Dakota." *American Anthropologist* 45 (1943): 67–83.

Goldschmidt, W., and R. B. Edgerton. "Picture Technique for the Study of Values." *American Anthropologist* 63 (1961): 26–47.

Goodman, Mary Ellen. *Race Awareness in Young Children.* Cambridge, Mass.: Addison-Wesley Press, 1952. 2d ed., enl. New York: Collier Books, 1964.

Graves, T. O. "The Personal Adjustments of Navajo Indian Migrants to Denver." In *Native Americans Today,* edited by Bahr, Chadwick, and Day. New York: Harper and Row, 1972. Pp. 440–66. Reprinted from *American Anthropologist* 72, no. 1 (1970).

———. "Values, Expectations and Relocation: The Navajo Migrant to Denver." *Human Organization* 25 (Winter 1965): 300–307.

Greenwald, Herbert J., and Don B. Oppenheim. "Reported Magnitude of Self Misidentification Among Negro Children—Artifact?" *Journal of Personality and Social Psychology* (1968): 49–52.

Gregor, James A., and D. A. McPherson. "Racial Preference and Ego Identity Among White and Bantu Children in the Republic of South Africa." *Genetic Psychology Monograph* 73 (1966): 218–53.

Grier, William, and Price Cobbs. *Black Rage.* New York: Basic Books, 1968.

Hallowell, A. Irving. "Impact of the American Indian on American Culture." *American Anthropologist* 59 (1957): 201–17.

Harris, Michael. "American Cities: The New Reservations." In *Cities.* Washington, D.C.: The National Urban Coalition, 1971. Pp. 45–48.

Harrison-Ross, Phyllis. *The Black Child: A Parent's Guide.* New York: Peter H. Wyden, 1973.

Havighurst, Robert, Minna Gunther, and Inez Ellis Pratt. "Environment and the Draw-a-Man Test: The Performance of Indian Children." *Journal of Abnormal and Social Psychology* 41 (1946): 50–63.

Havighurst, Robert, and Rhea Hilkevitch. "The Intelligence of Indian Children as Measured by a Performance Scale." *Journal of Abnormal and Social Psychology* 39 (1944): 419–33.

Helgerson, Evelyn. "The Relative Significance of Race, Sex and Facial Expression in Choice of Playmates by the Preschool Child." *Journal of Negro Education* 12 (1943): 617–22.

Henry, Jules. "Spontaneity, Initiative and Creativity in Suburban Classrooms." In *Education and Culture: Anthropological Approaches,* edited by George Spindler. New York: Holt, Rinehart and Winston, 1963. Pp. 215–34.

Henry, William. "Projective Tests in Cross-Cultural Research." In *Studying Personality Cross-Culturally,* edited by Bert Kaplan. New York: Harper and Row, 1968.

Hertzberg, Hazel W. *The Search for an American Indian Identity: Modern Pan Indian Movements.* Syracuse, N.Y.: Syracuse University Press, 1971.

Horowitz, Eugene, and Ruth Horowitz. "Development of Social Attitudes in Children." *Sociometry* 1 (1938): 301–38.

Horowitz, Ruth. "Racial Aspects of Self-Identification in Nursery School Children." *Journal of Psychology* 7 (1939): 91–99.

Houts, Kathleen, and Rosemary S. Bahr. "Stereotyping of Indians and Blacks in Magazine Cartoons." In *Native Americans Today,* edited by Bahr, Chadwick, and Day. New York: Harper and Row, 1972. Pp. 110–14.

Hraba, J., and G. Grant. "Black is Beautiful. A Re-Examination of Racial Attitudes." *Journal of Personality and Social Psychology* 16 (1970): 398–401.

Hurt, W. R., and R. M. Brown. "Social Drinking Patterns of the

Yankton Sioux." *Human Organization* 221 (1968): 222–30.

Hyde, George. *Red Cloud's Folk*. Norman, Oklahoma: University of Oklahoma Press, 1957.

Johnson, Helen W. "Rural Indian Americans In Poverty." In *Native Americans Today,* edited by Bahr, Chadwick, and Day. New York: Harper and Row, 1972.

Jones, James M. *Prejudice and Racism*. Reading, Mass.: Addison-Wesley, 1972.

Joseph, Alice M.D., Rosamond Spicer, and Jane Chesky. *The Desert People*. Chicago: University of Chicago Press, 1949.

Kaplan, Bert. "Cross-Cultural Use of Projective Techniques." In *Psychological Anthropology,* edited by Francis L. K. Hsu. Cambridge, Mass.: Schentzman Publishing Co., 1972.

Kardiner, Abram, and Lionel Ovesey. *The Mark of Oppression*. New York: Meridian Books, 1962.

Katz, Irwin, Thomas Henckey, and Harvey Allen. "Effects of Race of Tester, Approval-Disapproval and Need on Negro Children's Learning." *Journal of Personality and Social Psychology* 8 (1968): 38–42.

Katz, Irwin, James Robinson, Edgar Epps and Patricia Waly. "The Influence of Race of the Experimenter and Instructions Upon the Expression of Hostility by Negro Boys." *Journal of Social Issues* 20 (1964): 54–59.

Keller, Suzanne. "Social World of the Urban Slum Child." *American Journal of Orthopsychiatry* 33 (1963): 823–31.

Kerchoff, A. C. "Anomie and Achievement Motivation: A Study of Personality Development Within Cultural Disorganization." *Social Forces* 37 (1959): 196–202.

Koch, Helen. "The Social Distance Between Certain Racial, Nationality and Skin Pigmentation Groups in Selected Populations of American School Children." *Journal of Genetic Psychology* 68 (1946): 63–95.

Kohlberg, L., "A Cognitive-Developmental Analysis of Children's Sex-Role Concepts and Attitudes." In *The Development of Sex Differences,* edited by Eleanor Maccoby. Stanford, Cal.: Stanford University Press, 1974. Pp. 82–173.

———. "The Development of Moral Character and Ideology."

Review of Child Development Research, vol. 1, edited by M. and L. Hoffman. New York: Russell Sage, 1964.

Koslin, Sandra C., Marianne Amarel, and Nancy Ames. "The Effect of Race on Peer Evaluation and Preference in Primary Grade Children: An Exploratory Study." *Journal of Negro Education* 39 (1970): 346–50.

Krush, Thaddeus P., John W. Bjork, and Joanna N. Sindell. "Some Thoughts on the Formation of Personality Disorder: Study of an Indian Boarding School Population." *The American Journal of Psychiatry* 122 (1966): 868–76.

Landreth, Catherine, and B. C. Johnson. "Young Children's Response to a Picture and Inset Test Designed to Reveal Reactions to Persons of Different Skin Colors." *Child Development* 24 (1953): 65–79.

Lange, C. H. "Acculturation in the Context of Selected New and Old World Peasant Cultures." *American Anthropologist* 59 (1957): 1067–74.

Lasker, Bruno. *Race Attitudes in Children*. New York: Henry Holt and Company, 1929.

Leighton, Alexander H. "Introduction to the Mental Health of the American Indian." *American Journal of Psychiatry* 125 (1968): 217–18.

Leon, Robert L. "Some Implications For a Preventive Program For American Indians: The Mental Health of the American Indian." *American Journal of Psychiatry* 125 (1968): 128–32.

Lesser, A. "Education and the Future of Tribalism in the U.S." *Social Service Review* 35 (1961): 135–43.

Levine, Stuart, and Nancy L. Lurie. *The American Indian Today*. Baltimore: Penguin Books, 1970.

Levitan, Sar, and Barbara Hetrick. *Big Brother's Indian Programs: With Reservations*. New York: McGraw-Hill, 1971.

Levy, T. E., "Navajo Suicide." *Human Organization* 24 (1965): 308–18.

Lewin, Kurt. *Field Theory in Social Science: Selected Theoretical Papers*. New York: Harper and Brothers, 1951.

Liberty, Margot. "The Urban Reservation." Ph.D. dissertation, University of Minnesota, 1973.

Littlefield, D. F., and L. E. Underhill, "Negro Marshals in the Indian Territory." *Journal of Negro History* 56 (1971): 77–87.

Luebben, Ralph A. "Prejudice and Discrimination against Navajos in a Mining Community." In *Native Americans Today,* edited by Bahr, Chadwick, and Day. New York: Harper and Row, 1972. Pp. 89–101.

McDermott, Walsh, Kurt W. Deuschle and Clifford R. Barnett. "Health Care Experiment at Many Farms." *Science* 175 (7 January 1972): 23–31.

Macgregor, Gordon. *Warriors without Weapons.* Chicago: University of Chicago Press, 1946.

McNickle, D'Arcy. "The Sociocultural Setting of Indian Life: The Mental Health of the American Indian." *American Journal of Psychiatry* 125 (1968): 115–19.

Mangin, William, ed. *Peasants in Cities.* Boston: Houghton Mifflin Company, 1970.

Martin, Harry W. "Correlations of Adjustment Among American Indians in an Urban Environment." *Human Organization* 23 (1964): 290–95.

Martin, Harry W., et al. "Mental Health of Eastern Oklahoma Indians: An Exploration." *Human Organization* 27 (1968: 308–15.

Mason, Evelyn P. "Cross-Validation Study of Personality Characteristics of Junior High Students from American Indian, Mexican and Caucasian Ethnic Backgrounds." *Journal of Social Psychology* 77–78 (1969): 15–24.

———. "Personality Characteristics of Junior High Students From American Indian, Mexican and Caucasian Ethnic Backgrounds." *Journal of Social Psychology* 73 (1967): 145–55.

Mead, Margaret. *The Changing Culture of an Indian Tribe.* New York: Columbia University Press, 1932.

Mekeel, Scudder. *A Modern American Indian Community in the Light of Its Past: A Study in Cultural Change.* New Haven: Yale University Press, 1932.

Melzer, H. "The Development of Children's Nationality Preferences, Concepts and Attitudes." *Journal of Psychology*
11 (1941): 343–58.

———. "Nationality Preferences and Stereotypes of Colored
Children." *Journal of Genetic Psychology* 54 (1939): 403–
24.

Meriam, Lewis, et al. *The Problem of Indian Administration.*
Institute of Government Research. Baltimore: Johns Hopkins Press, 1928.

Merton, Robert K. *Social Theory and Social Structure.* Enl. ed.
New York: Collier-Macmillan, 1968. Pp. 215–48, 335–490.

Morland, Kenneth. "Comparison of Racial Awareness in
Northern and Southern Children." *American Journal of
Orthopsychiatry* 36 (1966): 22–32.

———. "Racial Recognition by Nursery School Children in
Lynchburg, Virginia." *Social Forces* 37 (1958): 132–37.

———. "Racial Self-Identification: A Study of Nursery School
Children in Lynchburg, Virginia." *American Catholic Sociological Review* 24 (1953): 373–76.

Nabokov, Peter. *Two Leggings.* New York: Thomas Crowell
Company, 1967.

Norman, R. D., and K. L. Medkeff: "Navajo Children on Raven
Progressive Matrices and Goodenough Draw-a-man
Tests." *Southwest Journal of Anthropology* 11 (1955):
129–36.

"Note on Indian Affairs." *Social Service Review* 31 (1959): 90.

Nurge, Ethel, ed. *The Modern Sioux: Social Systems and Reservation.* Lincoln: University of Nebraska Press, 1970.

Office of the Governor, State of Iowa. *Comprehensive Treatment Program for Indian Problem Drinkers.* Des Moines,
1972.

Ohiyesa. "First Impressions of Civilization." *Harpers* 108
(1903–1904): 587–92.

Palermo, David. "Racial Comparisons and Additional Norma-
tive Data on the Children's Manifest Anxiety Scale."
Child Development 30 (1959): 53–57.

Parker, Seymour. "Ethnic Identity and Acculturation in Two
Eskimo Villages." In *Native Americans Today*, edited by

Bahr, Chadwick, and Day. New York: Harper and Row, 1972. Pp. 261–75.

Parmee, Edward A. *Formal Education and Culture Change: A Modern Apache Community and Government Education Programs.* Tucson, Arizona: University of Arizona Press, 1968.

Pettigrew, Thomas. *Racially Separate or Together?* New York: McGraw Hill, 1971.

Piaget, J. *The Origins of Intelligence.* New York: International Universities Press, 1952.

——. *Psychology of Intelligence.* Trans. Malcolm Piercy and D. E. Berlyne. New York: Littlefield, Adams and Co., by arrangement with the Humanities Press, 1973.

Platero, Dillon. "Let's Do It Ourselves!" *School Review* 79, no. 1 (1970): 57–58.

Porter, Judith D. R. *Black Child, White Child.* Cambridge: Harvard University Press, 1971.

Poussaint, Alvin F. "Building a Strong Self-Image in the Black Child." *Ebony* (August 1974): 136–43.

Price, J. A. "Migration and Adaptations of American Indians to Los Angeles." *Human Organization* 27 (1968): 163–76.

Radke, Marion, Jean Sutherland, and Pearl Rosenberg. "Racial Attitudes of Children." *Sociometry* 13 (1950): 154–71.

Radke, Marion and Helen Trager. "Children's Perceptions of the Social Roles of Negroes and Whites." *Journal of Psychology* 29 (1950): 3–33.

Reasons, Charles. "Crime and the American Indian. In *Native Americans Today,* edited by Bahr, Chadwick, and Day. New York: Harper and Row, 1972. Pp. 319–26.

"Red and Black: Paradoxical Freedom Born of the Outsider." *Times Literary Supplement* 3010, Sup. XXVIII, no. 6: 59.

Reeder, T. A. "A Study of the Relationship Between Certain Aspects of Self Concept Behavior and Students' Academic Achievement." *Dissertation Abstracts* 16 (1956): 2531–32.

Rives, James A. "A Comparative Study of Traditional and Programmed Methods For Developing Music Listening

Skills." *Journal of Research in Music Education* 18 (Summer 1970): 126–33.

Rosenberg, Morris, and Roberta G. Simmons. *Black and White Self-Esteem.* Washington, D.C.: The American Sociological Association, 1971.

Rosenblatt, Joen B. "Measures of Impulse Control as Related to First-Grade Children's Socio-Economic Class and Ethnic Background." *Dissertation Abstracts* 29 (1968): 1510–11.

Rosenthal, Bernard. "Development of Self-Identification in Relationship to Attitudes Towards the Self in the Chippewa Indians." *Genetic Psychology Monographs* 90 (August 1974): 44–141.

Rotire, V. J. "Nutritional Factors in Windego Psychosis." *American Anthropologist* 72 (February 1970): 97–107.

Roy, Prodipto. "The Measurement of Assimilation: The Spokane Indians." *The American Journal of Sociology* 67 (March 1962): 541–51.

Russell, F. "The Pima Indians." *Annual Report of the Bureau of American Ethnology* XXVI. Washington, D.C.: Government Printing Office, 1908. Pp. 3–390.

Saslow, Harry L., and May S. Harrover. "Research on Psychosocial Adjustment of Indian Youth." *American Journal of Psychiatry* 125 (1968): 225–31.

Shaw, Anna Moore. *Pima Indian Legends.* Tucson: University of Arizona Press, 1968.

Sheehan, B. W. "Indian-White Relations in Early America." *William and Mary Quarterly* 26 (1969): 267–86.

Siever, Maurice. "Disease Patterns Among Southwestern Indians." *Public Health Reports.* December 1966.

Silberman, Charles. *Crisis in the Classroom.* New York: Random House, 1970.

Simpson, George, and Milton Yinger. *Racial and Cultural Minorities.* New York: Harper Brothers, 1958.

Sorkin, A. L. "Some Aspects of American Indian Migration." *Social Forces* 48 (December 1969): 243–50.

Sorkin, Alan L. *American Indians and Federal Aid.* Washington, D.C.: The Brookings Institution, 1971.

Spicer, Edward H. "Social Structure and the Culture Process in Vaqui River Religious Acculturation." *American Anthropologist* 60 (1958): 433–55.

Spindler, George D., and Louise S. Spindler. "Instrumental Activities Inventory: A Technique for the Study of Psychology of Acculturation." *Southwest Journal of Anthropology* 21 (1965): 1–23.

———. "American Indian Personality Types and Their Sociocultural Roots." *Annals of the American Academy of Political and Social Sciences* 311 (1957):147–57.

———. "A Modal Personality Technique in the Study of Menomini Acculturation." In *Studying Personality Cross-Culturally,* edited by Bert Kaplan. New York: Harper and Row, 1961. Pp. 479–92.

Springer, Doris. "Awareness of Racial Differences by Preschool Children in Hawaii." *Genetic Psychology Monographs* 41 (1950): 215–70.

Stabler, John R., E. Johnson, M. Berke, and Robert Baker. "The Relationship Between Race and Perception of Racially Related Stimuli in Pre-School Children." *Child Development* 40 (1969): 1233–39.

Steiner, Stan. *The New Indians.* New York: Dell Publishing Co., 1968.

Stember, Charles Herbert, et al. *Jews In The Mind of America.* New York: Basic Books, 1966.

Stevenson, Harold, and Edward Stevenson. "A Developmental Study of Racial Awareness in Children." *Child Development* 29 (1958): 399–409.

Stonequist, Everett. *The Marginal Man.* New York: Charles Scribner's Sons, 1937.

Tax, Sol. "Fox Project." *Human Organization* 17 (1958): 17–19.

Taylor, Charlotte P. "Some Changes in Self-Concept in First Year of Desegregation Schooling." *Dissertation Abstracts* 29 (1968): 821–22.

Thayer, J. B. "People Without Law." *Atlantic* 68 (1891): 540–51.

Thiel, Richard H. "An Analysis of Social-Culture Factors and Performance of Primary Grade Children." *Dissertation Abstracts* 29, 12A (1969): 4394.

Thomas, W. I. "The Psychology of Race Prejudice." *American Journal of Sociology* 9 (1904): 593–611.

Trager, Helen, Marion Radke, and Hadassah Davis. "Social Perceptions and Attitudes of Children." *Genetic Psychology Monographs* 40 (1949): 327–447.

Tunley, Roul. "Smooth Path at Rough Rock." In *American Education*. Washington, D.C.: U. S. Department of Health, Education and Welfare, March 1971. Pp. 15–20.

Underhill, Ruth. "The Papago Indians of Arizona and Their Relatives the Pima." Washington, D.C.: United States Bureau of Indian Affairs, Education Division, 1940.

U. S. Census of Population: 1960 (Nonwhite Population by Race). Department of Commerce. Washington, D.C.: Government Printing Office, 1963.

U. S. Department of Health, Education and Welfare, Office of the Secretary. *The Indian Health Program of the United States Public Health Service*. Washington, D.C.: Government Printing Office, 1966.

——. "Indian Poverty and Indian Health." *Indicators*, March 1964.

Van Duzen, Jean, et al. "Protein and Calorie Malnutrition Among Preschool Navajo Children." *Journal of Clinical Nutrition* 22 (1969): 1362–70.

Vaughan, Graham. "Concept Formation and the Development of Ethnic Awareness." *Journal of Genetic Psychology* 103 (1963): 93–103.

Vogel, F. W. "American Indian in Transition: Reformation and Accommodation." *American Anthropologist* 58 (1956): 249–63.

Waddell, J. O. "Resurgent Patronage and Lagging Bureaucracy in a Papago Off-Reservation Community." *Human Organization* 29 (1970): 37–42.

Wagner, Carruth J. "Federal Health Services For Indians and Alaska Natives." *The Journal Lancet* 84, no. 9 (1964).

Wahrhaftig, Albert L., and Robert K. Thomas. "Renaissance and Repression: The Oklahoma Cherokee." In *Native Americans Today*, edited by Bahr, Chadwick, and Day. New York: Harper and Row, 1972. Pp. 80–88.

Wallace, Helen M. "The Health of American Indian Children." *Health Services Reports* 87, no. 9 (1972): 867–76.

Wax, Murray L. *Indian Americans: Unity and Diversity*. Englewood Cliffs, N.J.: Prentice-Hall, 1971.

Wax, Murray, et al. "Formal Education in an American Indian Community." Supplement to *Social Problems* 2, no. 3 (1964).

Wax, Murray, and Rosalie Wax. "The Enemies of the People." In *Native Americans Today*, edited by Bahr, Chadwick, and Day. New York: Harper and Row, 1972. Pp. 177–92.

Wax, Rosalie. "The Warrior Dropouts." In *Native Americans Today*, edited by Bahr, Chadwick, and Day. New York: Harper and Row, 1972. Pp. 146–55.

Wax, Rosalie, and Robert K. Thomas. "American Indians and White People." In *Native Americans Today*, edited by Bahr, Chadwick, and Day. New York: Harper and Row, 1972. Pp. 31–41.

Webb, George. *A Pima Remembers*. Tucson: University of Arizona Press, 1959.

White, Lynn, and Bruce Chadwick. "Urban Residence, Assimilation and Identity of the Spokane Indian." In *Native Americans Today*, edited by Bahr, Chadwick, and Day. New York: Harper and Row, 1972. Pp. 239–49.

Whyte, William F. *Street Corner Society*. 2nd edition. Chicago: University of Chicago Press, 1955.

Williams, T. R. "Structure of the Socialization Process in Papago Indian Society." *Social Forces* 36 (1958): 251–56.

Wilson, Edmund. *Apologies to the Iroquois*. New York: Farrar, Straus & Giroux, 1960.

Winer, B. J. *Statistical Principles in Experimental Design*. New York: McGraw Hill, 1962.

Work Group for the Society for the Psychological Study of Social Issues. *SCC Journal of Social Issues*, 1969.

Zelegs, Ruth. "Children's Intergroup Attitudes." *Journal of Genetic Psychology* 72 (1948): 101–10.
——. "Racial Attitudes of Children." *Sociology and Social Research* 21 (1937): 361–71.
Zintz, M. V. "Problems of Classroom Adjustment of Indian Children in Public Elementary Schools in the Southwest." *Science Education* 46 (1962): 216–69.

Index

152

Index